MACBOOK
USER GUIDE

AN EASY, STEP-BY-STEP GUIDE ON MASTERING THE USAGE OF YOUR NEW MACBOOK. LEARN THE BEST TIPS & TRICKS, AND DISCOVER THE MOST USEFUL SECRETS TO GET THE MAX OUT OF YOUR DEVICE

BY
ETHAN COPSON

MACBOOK USER GUIDE © COPYRIGHT 2023

ALL RIGHTS RESERVED

ETHAN COPSON

Disclaimer

Limit of Liability/Disclaimer of Warranty: This publication is designed to provide accurate and authoritative information in regard to the subject matter covered. It is sold with the understanding that neither the author nor the publisher is engaged in rendering legal, investment, accounting or other professional services.

While the publisher and author have used their best efforts in preparing this book, they make no representations or warranties with respect to the accuracy or completeness of the contents of this book and specifically disclaim any implied warranties of merchantability or fitness for a particular purpose. No warranty may be created or extended by sales representatives or written sales materials.

The advice and strategies contained herein may not be suitable for your situation. You should consult with a professional when appropriate. Neither the publisher nor the author shall be liable for any loss of profit or any other commercial damages, including but not limited to special, incidental, consequential, personal, or other damages.

TABLE OF CONTENTS

TABLE OF CONTENTS

INTRODUCTION

No matter if you're switching from an old Mac to a new one, returning to macOS after a lengthy absence, or anything else, getting acclimated to a new machine may be a difficult process.

A range of laptop computers known as MacBooks was created and produced by Apple Inc. It is a well-known brand that is renowned for its svelte form, premium materials, and compatibility with Apple's macOS operating system. The dependability, performance, and user-friendly design of MacBooks are well known.

There are various different MacBook models, including the MacBook Air and MacBook Pro. Because of its mobility, extended battery life, and lightweight construction, the MacBook Air is popular for daily usage. The MacBook Pro, on the other hand, caters to professionals and power users who want higher processing capabilities for jobs like video editing, graphic design, and software development. It provides more potent hardware options.

Apple's iCloud, iMessage, FaceTime, and Continuity capabilities, which let users move smoothly between their MacBook and other Apple devices like iPhones and iPads, are just a few examples of how well-integrated MacBooks are with other Apple products and services.

In general, MacBooks are praised for their design, functionality, and the Apple ecosystem of programs and services. They have a devoted user base that values their elegant appearance, dependable performance, and the user-friendly interface of the macOS operating system.

Since they have been around for a while, MacBooks have established themselves as some of the most well-liked laptops on the market. They have some fantastic features, are beautifully made, and are simple to use. Why, then, are they so well-liked? More significantly, why are they superior than laptops with Windows operating systems?

Here, we'll go over a number of arguments for why we believe Apple laptops to be superior than those made by the competition, including topics like buying simplicity, durability, and more.

1. DESIGN AND SOCIAL IMAGE

Let's face it: The MacBook is awesome. Other laptop manufacturers strive (and fail) to mimic their clean appearance, and Apple has spent years elevating its brand's social image as exclusive and innovative.

When others see you carrying a MacBook, they are likely to assume you are imaginative, fashionable, and most likely successful. Of course, you can use any laptop to be all of those things. However, it cannot be denied that MacBooks have a certain social cachet that other laptops just do not.

2. EASE OF PURCHASE

There are two reasons why buying a MacBook is simpler than buying a Windows or Linux notebook.

They only have two varieties—MacBook Air and MacBook Pro—each with an own market niche. Making the best MacBook choice for you is made simpler by this condensed list of alternatives. Contrast this with other manufacturers' products, such as HP, which offer several variations of the same laptops with obscure names.

Second, Apple's retail stores are dispersed all over the world and staffed with experienced employees who can assist you in making your purchase. Apple's online shop is similarly structured and simple to use. In comparison, the websites of many other laptop manufacturers may be challenging to use, and their stores can be crowded and overwhelming.

3. LONGEVITY AND RESALE VALUE

The durability and value retention of MacBooks is one of their finest qualities. While many laptops can last you many years (or more), only MacBooks will remain fashionable after all that time and still command a respectable price on the used market.

Apps expand in size over time, and computers as a whole begin to run more slowly. But Apple is among the greatest firms for consistently providing fresh software upgrades for outdated devices. This not only protects you from security risks, but it also enables you to keep adding new features to your Mac as it becomes older.

The fact that MacBooks are so durable may be why they hold their value so well. A three-year-old MacBook may often be sold for about 50% of its original cost. But a Windows laptop from three years ago? If you were lucky, you may obtain 25% of the initial price.

4. QUALITY AND DURABILITY

Apple laptops are not just made of premium materials and hardware that leads the industry. A Mac may easily last you six years or longer with routine, modest upkeep. Simply taking good care of your Mac will enough.

Although there is fierce competition among numerous computers in this market, MacBooks dominate. They are strong and substantially more resistant to wear and tear thanks to their aluminum unibody construction (until you drop and ding them, of course).

Additionally, every product is covered by Apple's one-year guarantee, and repairs can be scheduled easily at the closest Apple Store.

5. MACOS AND APPS

The operating system for MacBooks is a significant selling element as well. The operating system that ships with MacBooks, macOS, is extremely dependable and user-friendly and was created especially for Apple's machines. Despite the widespread belief that macOS is not user-friendly, novice users believe macOS to be simpler to use than Windows.

Additionally, it has a number of built-in Mac programs that are compatible with all of your other Apple products. More excellent apps that are great for creativity, work, and fun may be found in the App Store.

6. THE MAGIC TRACKPAD

One of the nicest aspects of the MacBook is the Magic Trackpad. For a variety of reasons, its trackpad offers a seamless, responsive tracking experience that is unmatched by any other laptop on the market.

First of all, haptic feedback is the foundation of the Apple trackpad. Therefore, the trackpad employs magnets and motors to detect a click rather than buttons beneath its surface. Users may thus click anywhere on the trackpad, and it will be recognized. These days, several Windows laptop manufacturers use this style.

Second, the trackpad has a ton of built-in motions that, when used with the software, make managing your Mac really simple. For instance, you may engage Mission Control by swiping up or down with four fingers or pinching to zoom in or out practically anyplace.

Last but not least, the navigation is swift and simple because to the trackpad's gorgeous size and comfort. These days, the trackpads on most laptops from other companies are smaller because their main focus is on other functions.

7. THE IMMERSIVE EXPERIENCE

The superior audio, video, and typing experiences of MacBooks, which make them a more complete product, are another factor that makes them superior to competing Windows laptops. For instance, everything seems clearer on Macs because their Retina Displays have a greater pixel density than the majority of Windows laptop panels. Only extremely expensive Windows laptops have displays of this caliber.

Due to the scissor-switch keyboard's key travel and spacing, it is far more pleasant to type on than the keyboards on most Windows laptops.

The superior audio, video, and typing experiences of MacBooks, which make them a more complete product, are another factor that makes them superior to competing Windows laptops. For instance, everything seems clearer on Macs because their Retina Displays have a greater pixel density than the majority of Windows laptop panels. Only extremely expensive Windows laptops have displays of this caliber.

Due to the scissor-switch keyboard's key travel and spacing, it is far more pleasant to type on than the keyboards on most Windows laptops.

8. THE APPLE ECOSYSTEM

All of the hardware and software that Apple creates and releases are a part of the Apple ecosystem. The ecosystem includes almost all of Apple's hardware, software, and services, including the iPhone, iPad, Apple TV, Apple Watch, Mac, iCloud, Apple Music, and so forth.

Therefore, when people discuss the Apple ecosystem, they are really talking about how effectively all of these goods integrate. You may begin an activity (like reading an article) on your iPhone and continue where you left off on your Mac or iPad thanks to the ecosystem.

This seamless switching between Apple devices is a key reason why MacBooks are better than Windows laptops. While other laptop manufacturers have tried to create their own ecosystems, none of them have been as successful as Apple.

The unique benefits of the Apple ecosystem, thanks to the company's years of R&D in user experience, have resulted in MacBooks offering a more integrated and seamless experience than other laptops.

MACBOOKS VS. OTHER LAPTOPS: MAKE THE RIGHT CHOICE

There are several benefits to choosing a MacBook over other laptop types, such Windows or Linux computers, including their durability, resale value, design, and social standing. It is obvious why MacBooks are top items in their respective industries when you consider how simple they are to buy and the rich multimedia experience.

MacBooks vs. Other Laptops: Make the Right Choice

There are several benefits to choosing a MacBook over other laptop types, such Windows or Linux computers, including their durability, resale value, design, and social standing. It is obvious why MacBooks are top items in their respective industries when you consider how simple they are to buy and the rich multimedia experience.

But there are still some problems with MacBooks. The MacBook might not be the best choice for you, depending on what you want to do with it. Gaming is one such instance, when MacBooks aren't designed with gamers in mind.

HOW TO CHOOSE WHICH MAC IS BEST FOR YOU

I have advice for you if you haven't yet purchased a new Mac and are unsure which model to choose.

Any model of MacBook is what you'll desire if mobility is what you need. Looking for a compact, lightweight, and reasonably priced one? It's likely that you'll desire a MacBook Air. Need a portable device that is a little more powerful or perhaps has a bigger display? A MacBook Pro is what you need.

Avoid the portable alternatives and get a desktop model if you want to leave your Mac on the desk. The Mac mini could be the ideal option if all you need is a cheap replacement for a Windows desktop PC and you already have a great HDMI display. Or you may use an iMac if you want a straightforward all-in-one system with a stunning integrated display. You should get a Mac Studio if you are a power user with extremely high performance requirements (such as someone who works often with 4K video).

HOW TO SET UP UNIVERSAL CONTROL ON MAC

You must configure Universal Control on your Mac before you can use it. Note that only macOS Monterey 15.3 or later supports this capability.

From the Apple menu or the icon on the dock, access System Preferences.

Navigate to Displays.

Click the Advanced button at the bottom of the window.

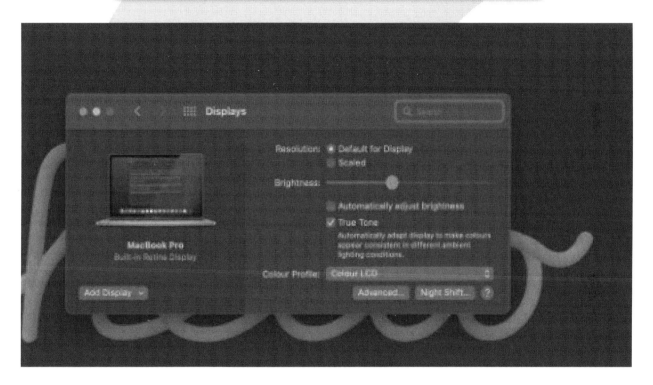

Check the boxes next to each item when the new page loads: Permit any adjacent Mac or iPad to move your cursor and keyboard. Connect a nearby Mac or iPad by pushing through the display's edge, and automatically reconnect to any nearby Mac or iPad.

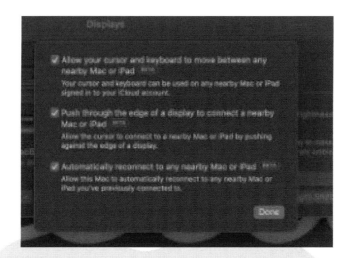

Then, select Done

Your Mac is now ready to work with other devices via Universal Control. But first, you'll need to configure those gadgets!

SET UP UNIVERSAL CONTROL ON IPAD

You must configure Universal Control on your iPad before you can use it. Note that only iPadOS 15.4 or later support this function.

From your home screen or the App Library, access Settings.

Go to General in the menu on the left.

After descending the list, select AirPlay& Handoff.

Turn on the option for the cursor and keyboard once you are on that page.

Your iPad is now prepared to use Universal Control.

After That?

The fun part has arrived now that Universal Control is set up—you can use it!

You must have your devices close to one another in order to use Universal Control. You won't be able to follow your cursor or keyboard if they are farther away. As I said above, you may utilize Universal Control with a maximum of three Mac and iPad devices.

CAN YOU USE UNIVERSAL CONTROL AND SIDECAR AT THE SAME TIME?

You can really use Universal operate to operate one device while using Sidecar to utilize the other as a display if you connect two devices simultaneously. For instance, in the configuration described in the instructions below, the primary machine is a desktop Mac, the secondary display is a laptop connected to Sidecar, and the iPad Pro is being used with Universal Control. The use of two iPads along with a Mac is also possible. Here's how to configure it.

- Integrate Universal Control across all of your devices.
- You will give responsibilities to the devices when Universal Control has been configured. The Displays system preference should be opened.
- To add a display, click. The list of available displays and their functions shows in a drop-down menu. You should utilize the devices listed in the Link Keyboard and Mouse section with Universal Control. Choose the gadget of your choice.
- Re-click Add Display. Look at the "Mirror or extend to" portion of the drop-down menu. You may use these as extra displays if you wish to. The iPads and Macs on this list work with Sidecar to provide your Mac an extra display. Choose the gadget of your choice.
- System preference Displays should be closed.

You ought to be prepared to depart. By clicking and dragging the icons for the displays' layouts at the top of the settings, you may adjust the Sidecar and Universal Control assignments and return to the Displays system options. By heading to the Home screen and touching the Sidecar app in the iPad's Dock, you can change the iPad's configuration from Sidecar to Universal Control if you have Sidecar installed.

SHOULD YOU USE UNIVERSAL CONTROL OR SIDECAR?

However, the majority of individuals will choose one over the other, and you can probably determine for yourself which is best for your requirements. If you're still unconvinced, think about the following instances:

- You favor using an iPad app over a Mac one.
- You have an iPad app without a Mac counterpart.

- You want to move data across devices but don't want to utilize an external storage device, a cloud storage service, or AirDrop.
- Managing one set of input devices makes it easier to utilize two Macs.
- You need to administer a different Mac or iPad while conducting hardware management.

You should utilize Universal Control if you meet any of those requirements. Even while it's still very new, it's a great feature that might start to blur the lines between the Mac and the iPad while still upholding the integrity of each device.

However, Sidebar is the way to go if you typically use a Mac and merely want to extend the desktop or utilize touch gestures. The Mac is typically the primary production tool, and it has all of your software tools. Having an extra display makes it much simpler to complete your task.

HANDOFF

On another Apple device, you may pick anything up exactly where you left it thanks to handoff. Imagine you're on your Mac drafting an email, but you have to go soon since you're running late. You may leave your email there and then and continue composing it on your iPhone with Handoff without any problems.

Handoff will continue sharing data across your Apple devices for applications like Mail, Safari, Maps, Messages, Reminders, Calendar, Contacts, Pages, Numbers, and Keynote as long as your devices remain synchronized with one another via iCloud.

This functionality is compatible with Macs running macOS Yosemite or later and iPhones running iOS 8 or later. The iPad (4th generation or later) and all Apple Watch devices support Handoff.

An Apple feature called handoff enables smooth switching between Apple devices without losing your place in an app or document.

An example is the best way to explain.

Imagine that you launch Mail on your iPad and begin responding to a significant message. You discover you need to attach a file from your Mac around halfway through. Instead of starting over from beginning, you may wirelessly transfer your partially written response from your iPad to your Mac using Handoff. Attach the file, then continue exactly where you left off.

Many different apps are compatible with Handoff, including:

- Pages
- Numbers
- Keynote

- Mail
- Calendar
- Contacts
- Reminders
- Safari
- Music
- Podcasts

and many third-party apps

In the exact same condition as it was on the first device, the app and document you were using open when you Handoff to a separate device.

The best approach to move music or podcast playback from one Apple device to another is through handoff. You can even copy something from your iPhone and paste it on your Mac using Handoff, or Universal Clipboard, to be more accurate.

Even an Apple Watch can be switched between using Handoff, but only from; not to. a Mac, iPhone, iPad, iPod touch, or other device.

HOW TO USE HANDOFF ON AN IPHONE, IPAD, OR MAC

Utilizing handoff is straightforward. Simply open a suitable app, begin using it on the first device, then adhere to the directions below to transfer the app to the second device.

If all you want to accomplish using Universal Clipboard is copy and paste between various devices, there is no extra action required. Simple copy and paste of material from one device to another.

HANDOFF TO AN IPHONE

To access the App Switcher, swipe up from the bottom of the screen (or, if your iPhone has one, double-click the Home button). Then click the banner at the bottom of the screen, which displays an app icon and identifies the source device.

HANDOFF TO AN IPAD

To find an app in the App Switcher view, use the iPhone technique described above, or go to the Home screen and press the app icon that shows on the Dock's far right side. It need to have a little badge that identifies the machine you're handing off from.

HANDOFF TO A MAC

When an app icon displays in the Dock, click it. This icon will show up at either the far left or far right edge of the Dock, depending on your version of macOS. It need to have a little badge that identifies the machine you're passing control of.

Alternately, you may use Cmd + Tab to open the App Switcher and choose the app that is on the left side. This app should include a badge that identifies the device you are passing control to.

FIX HANDOFF IF IT DOESN'T WORK

Compared to manually moving content between two devices, handoff is claimed to be simpler. The feature is generally effective, although rarely it malfunctions.

There are a number potential reasons why Handoff might not function properly, but by heeding the advice provided below, you should be able to resolve them.

SIGN IN TO THE SAME APPLE ID ACCOUNT ON BOTH DEVICES

Ensure that the same Apple ID or iCloud account is logged in on both devices you're attempting to utilize Handoff with.

- To verify this, open Settings on an iPhone or iPad and hit [Your Name] at the top of the screen.
- Open System Preferences on a Mac, then select Apple ID.
- Sign out of both devices, then sign back in if Handoff is still not working.

ENABLE HANDOFF IN THE SETTINGS ON BOTH DEVICES

One or both of the devices you're trying to use may have handoff disabled in its settings.

Go to Settings > General >AirPlay& Handoff on an iPhone or iPad, then turn on the Handoff feature.

Open the Apple Watch app on an iPhone that is connected, go to General, and choose Enable Handoff for an Apple Watch.

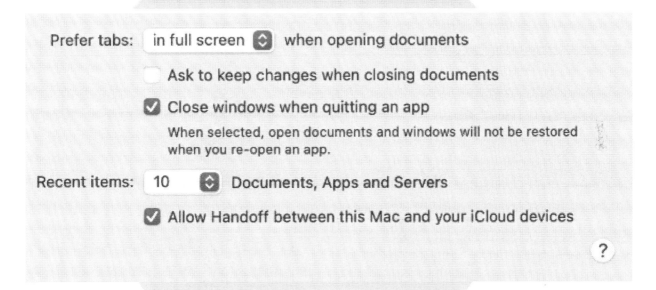

On a Mac, click General in the System Preferences window, choose Allow Handoff between this Mac and your iCloud devices, and then click OK.

Check to see if your device complies with Apple's website's Continuity criteria if you can't locate Handoff in the settings.

TURN ON WI-FI AND BLUETOOTH

Wi-Fi and Bluetooth are both used by handoff to transport data between your devices. Check that each device's Control Center has Bluetooth turned on before confirming that they are both connected to the same Wi-Fi network.

This is also a good opportunity to point out that for Handoff to function, both devices must be somewhat close to one another (or at least in the same room).

MAKE SURE THE APP IS OPEN ON THE FIRST DEVICE

The most frequent cause of Handoff issues is that the app you're attempting to transfer isn't running on the first device. Only the applications you're using at the moment can be handed over; none of your recent use counts.

This is especially important if you use music or podcast applications and listen to them in the background.

Make an app active on the first device you're using before handing it off. Try switching it over to another device once you open it and utilize it for a moment.

CONTINUITY CAMERA

One of the most intriguing Continuity features is perhaps the Continuity Camera, which Apple enhanced in 2022 with the release of the macOS Ventura update. Although there are many things you can do with it, the finest use cases would be utilizing the iPhone as a camera for your Mac and extending FaceTime chats across Apple devices.

In addition, images and documents you scan with your nearby iPhone or iPad will display right away on your Mac's screen.

Nearly all native applications that use the camera may be used with Continuity Camera. You can utilize this feature on iPhones running iOS 12 or later and Macs running macOS Mojave or later, but to use your iPhone as a camera, you'll need macOS Ventura.

USE CONTINUITY CAMERA TO REPLACE YOUR MAC'S CAMERA WITH YOUR IPHONE

There are a few requirements you need to confirm before you can begin using Continuity Camera. Both your Mac and iPhone must be running at least macOS Ventura and iOS 16, respectively. Both devices must be connected to the same Wi-Fi network and have Bluetooth turned on. It functions similarly to how Handoff between your Apple devices works.

You can utilize Continuity Camera now that it is over.

Launch FaceTime on your Mac computer.

After upgrading your macOS software to Ventura, you'll receive a welcome page outlining how Continuity Camera functions the first time you access FaceTime.

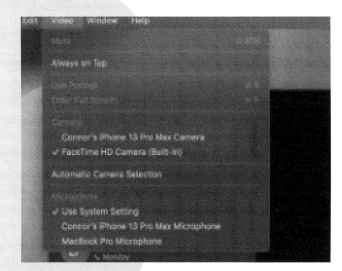

With the app open, head to the View tab in the menu bar.

Simply choose your iPhone from the list to replace your device's camera from here.

Your iPhone will display a message informing you that you are connected and taking up most of the screen. You can also choose to disconnect or pause the broadcast.

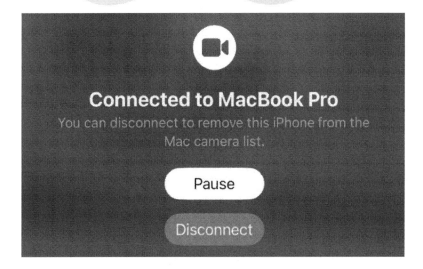

Your iPhone's camera will now serve as the webcam for your call.

You may return to the View tab after your call to resume using your Mac's camera. This is subject to change at any time.

If you're making a video call with a different program, such as Zoom, Google Meet, Microsoft Teams, etc. Go to the camera settings in the app once you're there. Choose your iPhone there instead of the built-in webcam. The automated process will function exactly the same manner.

USE VIDEO EFFECTS WITH CONTINUITY CAMERA

You may choose from a number of video effects in the Control Center while using a camera on a Mac. When utilizing Continuity Camera, you may keep employing these effects. A new Desk View option is also available, which provides a down-shot of the desk in front of you by utilizing the iPhone's ultra-wide lens and some ingenious image processing.

How to activate video effects is as follows:

By selecting the symbol in the menu bar, you may access the Control Center. You may accomplish this using any keyboard shortcuts or hand motions.

Click the Video Effects button at the top of the Control Center while it is open.

Click on the effect you wish to use from here.

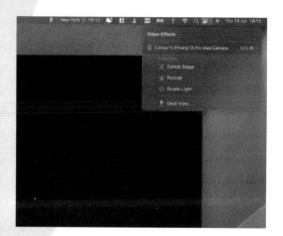

The camera feed will automatically adapt during your video conference to use the desired effect.

While Desk View is only accessible while using Continuity Camera, the majority of the video effect choices are also available on your Mac's camera.

APPLE PAY WITH IPHONE OR APPLE WATCH

A mobile payment and digital wallet service created by Apple is called Apple Pay. It enables you to use your Apple devices to pay in stores, applications, and online.

It's easy and safe to make purchases with Apple Pay on an iPhone or Apple Watch. You need an Apple Watch 3 or later running watchOS 6 or later in order to utilize Apple Pay on your Apple smartphone. Additionally, you must have an iPhone 6 or later running iOS 11 or above.

SYNCING YOUR MAC AND YOUR DEVICES

Syncing is the process of moving data between your Mac and your iPhone, iPad, or iPod touch and keeping them current. For instance, you may sync your Mac and iPhone so that a movie you add on your Mac will also display on your iPhone. Music, movies, TV shows, podcasts, books, and more may all be synced.

An iPhone, iPad, or iPod touch that is connected to your Mac through a USB or USB-C connection shows up in the Finder sidebar. The Finder window shows choices for configuring your device software and synchronizing objects with your Mac when you pick the device in the sidebar.

To enable synchronization for each form of material, such as music, movies, or TV shows, utilize the button bar across the top of the window.

For control over the data and software on your device, click General in the button bar. You can, for instance:

- For your iPhone, iPad, or iPod touch, search for the most recent software and install it.
- Your device's data should be backed up to iCloud or your Mac.
- Manage numerous backups if necessary and restore data from a backup onto your device.

DO I HAVE TO SYNC?

You must sync your iPod with your Mac if you have an iPod classic, iPod nano, or iPod shuffle. Nothing further can be done to add material to it.

You only need to sync with your Mac when you have new or updated material if you have an iPhone, iPad, or iPod touch.

You are under no obligation to sync your iPhone, iPad, or iPod Touch. You may download things to your devices straight from the iTunes Store, the App Store, Apple Books, and other Apple services. Additionally, you may use iCloud to maintain consistency across all of your devices.

SHOULD I CHOOSE TO AUTOMATICALLY SYNC ALL MY CONTENT OR ONLY SPECIFIC ITEMS?

All content should be automatically synced; this is the quickest and simplest method. Simply enable synchronization for each type of content you wish to sync by checking the "Automatically sync when this [device] is connected" box in the General pane. Anytime you connect your iPhone, iPad, or iPod touch to your Mac, the devices receive updates with the same material.

Sync certain things: You have the option to sync only certain objects. You might, for instance, sync only some movies on your iPhone to conserve storage. For other sorts of material, including podcasts, TV series, and novels, you can still automatically sync all things.

DO I HAVE TO CONNECT MY IPHONE, IPAD, OR IPOD TOUCH TO MY MAC TO SYNC?

No. When your Mac and your iOS-enabled iPhone or iPad are both connected to the same Wi-Fi network, you may sync your devices. You must first connect your device with a cable, choose it from the sidebar, then enable the syncing via Wi-Fi option before you can configure Wi-Fi syncing. See Sync material via Wi-Fi from your Mac to your iPhone, iPad, or iPod touch.

WHAT'S THE DIFFERENCE BETWEEN USING ICLOUD AND SYNCING?

You can easily and automatically move files between your Mac and iPhone, iPad, or iPod touch when you utilize iCloud. For instance, if you capture a photo on your iPhone using iCloud Photos, it will shortly show on your Mac and other devices. Your Mac, iPhone, iPad, or iPod touch are automatically updated as content changes when iCloud is enabled, and you don't have to do anything. To learn more, go to What Is iCloud?

To organize the files on your device, use syncing: By syncing, you may keep your device up to date with the most recent versions of iOS and iPadOS, safely backup your device's data to your Mac or the iCloud, and, if necessary, utilize a backup to recover data from your device.

You have excellent control over the content that is sent to your device when you sync. You can sync all or just a certain group of files. For instance, you may sync a number of audiobooks on your iPhone before a trip so that you can listen to them while driving. You may quickly transmit only the files you need using synchronization.

CHAPTER ONE
STAYING CONNECTED

WIRELESS CONNECTIVITY OPTIONS

WI-FI

There are internal wireless adapters inside every Apple MacBook model, including the MacBook Pro and MacBook Air. These are known as AirPort adapters. Connect your computer to a Wi-Fi router or access point using the AirPort adapter that came with your MacBook. From there, you can access the Internet from any location that has a strong enough signal. Apple places the icon for the MacBook's AirPort functionality on the top menu bar of the desktop because getting online is a basic requirement for any computer.

- On the desktop, click the AirPort icon in the top-right corner. An array of circular waves can be seen in the AirPort icon. Resulting in a pull-down menu.
- Then, select "Turn AirPort on." The AirPort adapter on your MacBook is already active if this option is not visible. The MacBook periodically scans for broadcasts from nearby Wi-Fi access points while the AirPort adapter is turned on. The names of all discovered access points are listed in the pull-down menu.
- To connect to a Wi-Fi access point, click its name. If you can't find your access point on the list, look under "Tips". The MacBook automatically joins the access point if it is unprotected. The MacBook will ask you to enter the encryption key if the access point uses one.
- Enter the encryption key for the access point. To connect, click the "Join" button.

MAC WON'T CONNECT TO WI-FI?

It's usually simple to connect your Mac to a Wi-Fi network. You select the network you want to join by clicking the Wi-Fi icon, then, if necessary, type the network password. This process might not always go as expected, though. Even if your Mac refuses to connect properly, I'll show you how to connect it to a Wi-Fi network.

CONFIRM PROPER NETWORK OPERATION

As the first step in troubleshooting, make sure your Wi-Fi network is operational. Attempting to connect with other devices is the simplest way to achieve this.

You'll know your Mac is to blame if another device is able to connect. However, if additional devices are unable to connect to the internet, your Wi-Fi network may be having issues.

Try these suggestions if your Wi-Fi network isn't operating properly:

- You should try restarting the WiFi router first. Turn it off, wait a few seconds, and then turn it back on. This will usually solve the problem.
- Make sure the cables connecting your router are connected correctly next. If so, try connecting the router using a different cable as the one you're currently using might be defective.
- You should try contacting your internet service provider (ISP) if neither of these options works. Maybe your area is experiencing a network outage. When you contact your ISP, they can look into it and, if necessary, send an engineer.

CHECK RANGE AND INTERFERENCE

Make sure your Mac isn't too far from the router when using Wi-Fi. Likewise, confirm that the location of your router is appropriate. It ought to be put away from barriers like thick walls. It's best to place it in the middle of your home or apartment; stay away from placing it on the edge.

Make sure there are no other types of interference with your router. Avoid placing it close to electrical cables, cordless phones, video cameras, microwaves, or other devices that could send out electrical signals.

Additionally, some users claim that turning off Bluetooth can be beneficial because Bluetooth signals may conflict with Wi-Fi.

UPDATE MACOS

When you experience system issues, it is always a good idea to check for software updates. Upgrade your Mac's operating system if a newer version is available and see if that solves your issue.

If you use macOS Ventura, follow these instructions to update your computer:

- Select System Settings from the dropdown menu under Apple menu.
- Click Software Update on the right after choosing General in the left pane.

- The Mac will look for updates.
- Click Update Now if there is an update available.

FORGET YOUR WI-FI NETWORK

Making your Mac forget the Wi-Fi network that's giving you problems is another step in the troubleshooting process.

Open your Mac's network preferences to do this, as shown below:

- On your Mac, select System Preferences.
- Click Advanced on the right after choosing Wi-Fi in the left pane.
- Look down at the list of Known Networks.
- Remove From List can be selected by clicking the more icon, which is represented by three dots inside a circle.

After that, you'll need to manually reconnect to the Wi-Fi network. Therefore, select the desired network by clicking the Wi-Fi icon on the right side of the menu bar.

CHECK YOUR TCP/IP SETTINGS

How your Mac interacts with other devices is determined by its TCP/IP configuration. Therefore, if your Mac won't connect to Wi-Fi, it's worth checking them. Renewing your DHCP (Dynamic Host Configuration Protocol) lease in particular can fix your connection. That's because it's in charge of giving your Mac an IP address.

These steps will renew it:

- Connect a Wi-Fi network connection.
- Open System Settings, choose Network, and then select Wi-Fi.
- Select TCP/IP in the following window after opening Details on the WiFi to which you are currently connected.
- Simply select Renew DHCP Lease.
- Press the blue Apply button when the prompt appears.
- To close the sub-window, click OK.

RUN WIRELESS DIAGNOSTICS

A wireless diagnostics tool included with macOS can be used to check your Mac's wireless services and produce a report.

Search for Wireless Diagnostics in Spotlight (Cmd + Space) to launch it. When you follow the on-screen instructions, a log will be produced that you can use to troubleshoot the issue with an IT expert or your internet service provider.

BLUETOOTH

You should be able to pair a variety of devices with your Mac using Bluetooth, which is a feature that is present on all modern Macs. It's a straightforward feature, but if you're not familiar with it, some aspects might be challenging. Let's examine how to activate Bluetooth on a Mac and what to do next. Let's look at how to confirm that your Mac is Bluetooth-compatible, where to enable the feature, and the fundamentals of pairing a new device.

DOES MY MAC HAVE BLUETOOTH?

Bluetooth support is pre-installed on all current Mac computers (made available in 2011 or later). For your MacBook Pro, MacBook Air, or iMac to support Bluetooth, you don't need to purchase any additional hardware.

To enable Bluetooth on your Mac and begin using it, just follow the steps below. Your Mac probably doesn't have Bluetooth if you don't see the pertinent Bluetooth options in the System Preferences panel.

In this situation, you might be able to buy an adapter that gives your computer support for Bluetooth. Make sure you choose one that is listed as compatible with macOS because the majority of these are created for Windows.

If your Mac is so outdated that it no longer supports Bluetooth, you should think about getting a new one. With outdated models like these, Bluetooth support is one of many issues.

HOW TO TURN ON BLUETOOTH ON MAC

Using Bluetooth on a Mac is simple, but you must first enable it. Open System Preferences from the Apple menu in the top-left corner of the screen to enable Bluetooth. Select Bluetooth from the ensuing window.

The Bluetooth icon and its current status are located on the left side of the Bluetooth panel. If Bluetooth is disabled, turn it on by clicking the Turn Bluetooth On button.

On a Mac, that is all it takes to activate Bluetooth. If it isn't already turned on, I suggest checking the Show Bluetooth in menu bar box while you're here. When you do this, a Bluetooth icon will appear at the top of your screen, allowing you to access Bluetooth connections without constantly entering this panel.

HOW TO CONNECT BLUETOOTH DEVICES TO YOUR MAC

Let's look at how to connect devices to your Mac now that Bluetooth is turned on. You must pair a Bluetooth device with your Mac before using it for the first time. Discoverability is a concept you should be familiar with if you've used Bluetooth on other devices in the past.

You must manually pair devices for security reasons because it's typical for numerous Bluetooth devices to be close together. And only when the device is discoverable (also referred to as being in "pairing mode") can you do this. Your computer is discoverable when the Bluetooth settings panel is open on your Mac, as previously mentioned.

PAIRING NEW BLUETOOTH DEVICES TO YOUR MAC

Depending on the device you want to pair, there are different Bluetooth pairing procedures in macOS. When you have the Bluetooth options page open, the majority of other operating systems—including Windows, Android, and iOS—set themselves as discoverable. The precise procedure to enter pairing mode varies depending on the device for those without a user interface, such as Bluetooth keyboards, mice, headphones, and similar items.

Usually, this entails pressing and holding the Power button for a few seconds or pressing a few buttons at once. For more details, consult the user guide for your gadget. When your other device is ready to pair, you should see its name under Devices in your Mac's Bluetooth settings. Next to the person you want to add, click the Connect button.

You must verify that the PIN entered on both devices matches for many Bluetooth devices. Check that this is accurate, particularly if you're in a crowded place with lots of gadgets. When entering a PIN manually (which usually only applies to older devices), use a standard sequence like 0000, 1111, or 1234.

You've now successfully used Bluetooth to pair your Mac with the other device. They will automatically connect once they are both turned on and within range of one another (roughly 30 feet). As a result, you don't have to go through the pairing procedure again each time you want to use the same device.

If your devices do not connect automatically, you can always connect them manually. Any previously paired devices appear under Devices in the Bluetooth settings panel (as well as the menu bar icon shortcut). To connect to a device, make sure it is turned on and then double-click its name. If this does not work, first disconnect the paired device from any other paired computers. Most Bluetooth devices will have issues when used with multiple devices at the same time, though the latest Bluetooth standards are working to address this.

To remove a device from the list, right-click it and select Remove. After you do this, the device will no longer connect automatically; you will need to pair it again before you can use it.

UNDERSTANDING THE MACOS BLUETOOTH ICON

If you've enabled the Bluetooth menu bar icon, as previously mentioned, you'll always see the Bluetooth logo there. You can use it to quickly turn on or off Bluetooth, connect to a device, or open the full preferences panel.

The icon will change depending on the status of Bluetooth. A simple icon indicates that Bluetooth is turned on. Meanwhile, if Bluetooth is turned off, the Bluetooth logo will have a slash through it. Other visual changes were made to the Bluetooth icon in previous versions of macOS to communicate useful information. Unfortunately, Apple removed these with the release of macOS Big Sur.

When you have at least one Bluetooth device connected to your Mac, you'll see the Bluetooth icon with three dots over it on older versions of macOS. When there is a Bluetooth issue, you may also see a zigzag line over the icon. If you see this, restart your Mac, and then go through Bluetooth troubleshooting.

TURNING ON BLUETOOTH ON YOUR MAC WITHOUT A MOUSE OR KEYBOARD

For their desktop Mac, many people use a Bluetooth mouse and/or keyboard. As you might expect, having Bluetooth suddenly turned off can cause issues here because you need those devices to access the Bluetooth menu.

Fortunately, macOS does not disable Bluetooth on Macs without a trackpad unless a USB mouse is connected. If your Mac does not detect a keyboard or mouse, it should display the Bluetooth Setup Assistant. However, if something goes wrong with those tools, you can re-enable Bluetooth on your Mac using only a mouse or a keyboard.

The built-in keyboard and trackpad on a MacBook make this a non-issue. On an iMac, however, you'll need to connect a USB mouse or keyboard to accomplish this. To enable Bluetooth without using a mouse, open Spotlight search by pressing Cmd + Space. To launch Bluetooth File Exchange, search for it and press Return. When you launch the app, a window will appear informing you that Bluetooth is disabled.

Return to accept the prompt to enable Bluetooth. If you need to access the Bluetooth panel, open Spotlight again and type System Preferences, then use the search box in that menu to look for Bluetooth. If you don't have a keyboard nearby, use your mouse to navigate to the Bluetooth menu bar icon or System Preferences panel.

AIRDROP

Since its debut in 2011, there has been a lot written about AirDrop. AirDrop was a brilliant addition to the Apple ecosystem nearly a decade ago. It lingered, languished, and eventually fell behind many competing services.

The criticism was valid at the time, but it is no longer true. Apple has made AirDrop faster to load and recognizes devices far better than it used to in recent years. I'll show you how to enable AirDrop on your Mac and other devices, as well as some apps that make file transfers effortless.

HOW DOES AIRDROP WORK?

The goal of AirDrop is straightforward: to transfer files. It detects nearby devices that can accept file transfers via WiFi and Bluetooth. You can accept files from anyone or just those on your contact list. You can also instruct AirDrop to block all incoming file transfers; however, doing so will render your device unreachable by others, preventing you from sending files.

AirDrop on the Mac entered a new era with OS X Yosemite. AirDrop for Mac and iOS were not interoperable prior to this version of OS X (now macOS). This made transferring files between a Mac and an iPhone or iPad difficult; however, this is no longer an issue now that these systems work well together.

Where can I find AirDrop on the Mac and iPhone? This is a common question among users, but it's not easy to answer because AirDrop isn't available as a standalone app. To share a file via AirDrop, simply select AirDrop from the share-sheet when right-clicking on a file or folder, then select AirDrop. A list of available devices to share with will appear.

HOW TO TURN ON AIRDROP ON MAC

AirDrop may not work on all devices, but it is built into Apple products. Let's take a look at how to enable AirDrop on Mac. While AirDrop is a very simple and effective sharing method, Apple does not make it readily available on the Mac. Here's how to enable AirDrop on a Mac:

- Open the Finder app on your Mac
- Select "AirDrop" from the Favorites section on the left side of the window.
- When you launch AirDrop on Mac, select the discoverability option that best suits you at the bottom of the window.

Note: If you select "Everyone" from this list, any Apple device in your vicinity will be able to send you files. Keep this in mind when you're out in public.

AirDrop can be a security risk because it allows anyone to send files to your Mac, iPhone, or iPad. If you receive a file or link containing malware, it may end up on your device without your knowledge!

HOW TO AIRDROP FROM MAC TO IPHONE

The Dropzone app is the quickest way to airdrop from Mac to iPhone. Simply begin dragging an image or a collection of images. The Dropzone icon will appear. Drop your image(s) to the AirDrop icon in Dropzone, and the image will be sent to your iPhone.

When using a Mac to send files to iPhones or iPads, another option is to right-click. This is how it's done:

- Locate the file you want to send to an iPhone
- In the new sub-menu, select "AirDrop"
- Right-click on the filename or thumbnail
- From the drop-down menu, scroll down to "Share"
- In the new window that appears, select the device you want to send a file or folder to.

AIRDROP A WORD, EXCEL, OR POWERPOINT FILE

When working in Word, Excel, or PowerPoint, you may want to AirDrop your file directly from the app so you don't have to waste time searching for it in Finder. It is simple:

- In Word, Excel, or PowerPoint, locate and click the Share button.
- You will be given sharing options. Select "Send a Copy"
- In a new window, click the sharing icon and select AirDrop.
- When a window with nearby devices appears, select the device to which you want to AirDrop your file.

HOW TO AIRDROP FROM IPHONE TO MAC

Next, let's look at how to AirDrop to a laptop. Sending files via AirDrop is a little different on iOS and iPadOS. This is how it's done:

- Select the image, file, webpage, or other item you want to share.
- Select the "share sheet" - a box icon with an upward-facing arrow - from the bottom of the screen.
- Choose "AirDrop" from the menu. Note: If the device you want to send the file to has AirDrop enabled and your device can send files to it as a contact, it may appear on the top row.
- Choose the Mac to which you want to send the file.

WHY AIRDROP IS NOT WORKING ON MY MAC

When using AirDrop on your Mac, there are a few things to look for, especially if you're having issues. Here are a few things to think about:

Your Mac is old. Does AirDrop work on older Macs? Yes, but not as well as more recent Macs. This can be an issue if you have an older Mac that doesn't support AirDrop or are running an older version of macOS than Yosemite. If you have an older Mac, the AirDrop protocol may no longer be compatible with your devices.

Your Mac's settings are turned off. When using AirDrop, keep in mind that you have three options: accept files from everyone, accept files from contacts, or do not accept AirDrop files at all. You can't send or receive files if your AirDrop settings are set to "No One," as I mentioned earlier.

Your iPhone or iPad's settings are incorrect. iPhones and iPads, like Macs, have three options for AirDrop. If you can't send or receive from any of these devices, check the AirDrop settings on each one.

The device does not function as a contact. When you set your AirDrop to "Contacts Only," it will only accept AirDrop files from people on your contact list. It's possible that your device isn't using an account associated with any of your contacts. Your Mac would not recognize a contact if your work phone used a work email as its account but that email wasn't listed in your contacts card in Settings. This can be an issue with new devices as well.

Bluetooth and WiFi are not functioning properly. AirDrop sends and receives files via Bluetooth or WiFi. If you're on the same WiFi network, you shouldn't have any problems unless it's public WiFi or something is preventing your devices from connecting (a VPN, for example). It's also a good idea to turn on Bluetooth on both devices.

FACETIME, IMESSAGE, AND OTHER COMMUNICATION TOOLS

You can set up your Mac to receive calls and texts from your iPhone if, like me, you would rather type on your laptop's keyboard than the tiny iPhone keypad or if you simply don't want to switch devices to answer a text or call. You can use the Messages and FaceTime apps on your Mac to send texts and make calls online with an Apple ID.

Your iPhone must be running iOS 8.1 or later, and your Mac must be running OS X Yosemite or later in order to make calls using cellular service or send SMS messages through your carrier rather than the internet.

Note: Your contacts won't be transferred between your Mac and iPhone if you follow these instructions. You'll need to either set up iCloud contacts or sync them to accomplish that.

SIGN IN TO IMESSAGES WITH YOUR APPLE ID

First, confirm that you have the same Apple ID signed into Messages on both your Mac and your iPhone. This is how:

Go to on your iPhone to check your Apple ID. "Settings" > "Messages" > "Send & Receive"

Open the Messages app on your Mac to check your Apple ID. Select "Preferences" from the drop-down menu after clicking "Messages" in the menu bar. Select "iMessage" from the window's top menu.

SET UP TEXT MESSAGE FORWARDING

To configure your Mac to receive SMS messages from your phone:

- Tap "Text Message Forwarding"
- On your iPhone, open up Settings
- Scroll down and go to "Messages"
- Toggle on the switch next to your laptop's name

SET UP FACETIME AND ICLOUD

Ensure that your Mac and iPhone are both signed into FaceTime and iCloud using the same Apple ID, and that both are connected to the same Wi-Fi network. This is how:

On your iPhone, tap "Settings." Your Apple ID ought to be visible at the very top of the settings window. To find out which account is active, scroll down and click "FaceTime".

On your Mac, click the Apple icon in the upper-left corner of the screen and choose "System Preferences." Verify that you are logged into the appropriate Apple account. Open the FaceTime app, select "FaceTime" from the drop-down menu in the top menu bar, and then choose "Preferences" from the list. You can see which account you are signed into at the top of the window.

ALLOW CALLS ON OTHER DEVICES

On your iPhone, you must now turn on a few settings:

> Tap "Phone" after opening Settings on your iPhone.
>
> Select "Calls on Other Devices"
>
> "Allow Calls on Other Devices" should be toggled on.
>
> As long as your Mac is turned on, make sure you are in "Calls on Other Devices."

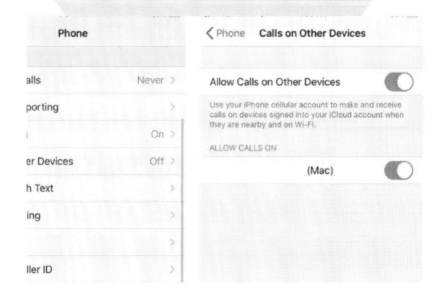

Launch the FaceTime program on your Mac.

Choose "Preferences" from the drop-down menu that appears when you click "FaceTime" in the menu bar at the top of the screen.

Choose "Settings" from the pop-up menu.

The "Calls from iPhone" checkbox should be selected.

Remember that your devices must be close to one another and connected to the same Wi-Fi network in order for you to receive calls from your phone. Use Wi-Fi calling on your Mac to take calls while it's connected to a different Wi-Fi network.

SET UP WI-FI CALLING

You can enable Wi-Fi Calling to make calls over the internet rather than cellular service if your Mac, phone (iPhone 5S or later), and carrier all support it. Depending on your carrier, you can also make calls when your phone is off and from devices that are not connected to the same Wi-Fi networks as your phone.

- Choose "Wi-Fi Calling" under "Settings" > "Phone" on your iPhone.
- Switch on "Wi-Fi Calling on This iPhone." You will be informed in a pop-up window how it sends location information to your carrier. Select "Enable."

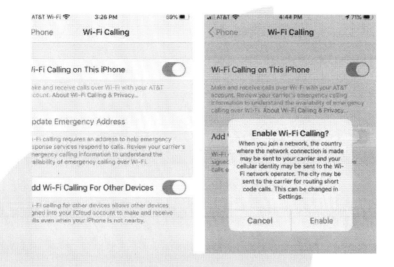

- Flip the switch to "Add Wi-Fi Calling For Other Devices." If you call 911 using Wi-Fi Calling, your carrier may use your automatic location data or the emergency address saved in your settings to route the call to an emergency response center. This information may be included in a message you receive from your carrier about Wi-Fi Calling, billing, and 911 calls. At the bottom of the notice, click "Continue".
- If location information is unavailable, you must give an address when making emergency calls. If your carrier has already stored an address for you (like your billing address), you can change it by selecting the blue "Update Emergency Address" button in the screen's center and following the on-screen instructions.

YOU MUST NOW SET UP YOUR MAC.

After enabling Wi-Fi calling on your phone, you might receive a notification on your Mac. When you click "Turn On," you'll either be taken to the Preferences window or the main FaceTime menu, depending on your situation. A smaller window will appear to let you know that your location will be shared with emergency callers. To approve this, click "OK".

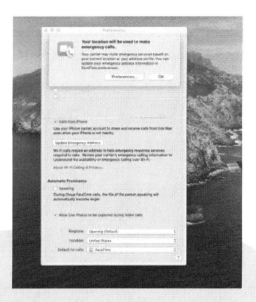

- Open FaceTime on your Mac, click FaceTime in the menu bar, and select "Preferences" from the drop-down menu if you don't see the notification.

- Ensure that "Settings" is selected at the window's top.

- When Wi-Fi Calling is available on your device, a button labeled "Upgrade to Wi-Fi Calling" will appear under the heading "Calls from iPhone." Just click it.

- You'll see a pop-up window warning you that your carrier may be given access to your location. To proceed, select "Enable".

Contact address for emergencies is also required here. This button will be replaced with one that reads "Update Emergency Address" after you click "Update to Wi-Fi Calling." To view and, if necessary, modify your address, click that.

You're done now!

STAYING PRODUCTIVE WITH MACOS PRODUCTIVITY FEATURES, MANAGING FILES AND ORGANIZING DATA EFFECTIVELY

Macs have many appealing qualities, including their minimalist design and hassle-free operation. However, when a mac user's computer begins to accumulate files and becomes cluttered, it can drive them crazy.

This may cause your Mac to lag and make it challenging to locate the necessary file. Let's talk about some Mac file organization best practices to keep your virtual space clutter-free and boost your productivity!

NAMING AND VIEWING YOUR FILES

Let's build things up from scratch. By precisely how you keep files on your Mac, that is. To recognize and access them quickly, it's crucial to create an efficient file system. Therefore, our first piece of advice for organizing files on a Mac is to name your files more precisely. To make file searches easier in the future, give file names details like dates, project names, and version numbers. You could even add a brief description.

Also, keep in mind all the different ways Finder offers you to view your files:

To sort files by name, file size, modified date, and other criteria, use the Finder's Sort By feature.

- Utilize Finder's search feature to perform a file type search and include file extensions in your search. For instance, you can type ".key" into the search bar to find a Keynote presentation.
- Press the spacebar while the file is selected to see a preview without opening it.

You can easily find and group files by using these suggestions.

SAVING YOUR FILES

Additionally, I advise using "Save as" more frequently than "Save". Even though this will involve a few more clicks, it will ultimately save time. Choosing "Save as" eliminates the need to move files from your downloads or documents folder to more appropriate folders where they should have been all along.

Simply press Command + Shift + S to open the Save As window, where you can give your file a name and specify where it should be saved.

MAC FOLDER STRUCTURE BEST PRACTICES

Most people are familiar with how to create folders, but are you effectively using them to organize your files? It can be tempting to simply throw everything into the same folder when you have all these files. But in the long run, this will only cause more issues. In order to organize files on a Mac, I advise using the following best practices:

GROUP BY FILE TYPE

Make distinct folders for your documents, music, videos, and pictures. This will make finding the necessary files quick and easy for you because you will know exactly where to look for a particular kind of file.

USE FOLDERS FOR DIFFERENT PROJECTS

You should be extremely specific about the function of each folder if you frequently work on several projects at once. For each project, you might want to make a folder and put the necessary files inside. Set up separate folders for files related to your job and passion projects. You can maintain focus by organizing your files by media and purpose to avoid mingling different files and concepts.

RELOCATE BACKUPS AND OLD VERSIONS

Consider creating a separate folder for backups and older versions of files in order to quickly "declutter" your main folders. By doing this, you can find the most recent versions of your files and free up space. You can simply delete the entire folder once you're certain you don't need these backups any longer. more room for storage.

USE IMAGES AS FOLDER ICONS

Although assigning images to serve as folder icons may seem a little extra, doing so can actually increase productivity. Using an image as a folder icon can make it easier for you to find the folder you're looking for because we process images more quickly than text. If you have a lot of folders with similar names, this is especially useful. Use these steps to designate an image as a folder icon:

On your Mac, select the image file you wish to use, then copy its contents to the Clipboard. When using a photo as a folder icon, make sure it is high definition and doesn't appear blurry. Control-click the folder in Finder to which you want to add the image, and then select Get Info from the shortcut menu. In the Get Info window, click the tiny folder icon at the top of the informational window.

Once the image has been pasted, press Command-V. Drag an image file into the folder icon to accomplish the same thing. Now, the icon for that folder will be the image. Just click the folder icon and press Command + X to restore the original folder icon.

MAC FILE ORGANIZATION USING SMART FOLDERS

One of the most creative and underappreciated Mac features is Smart Folders. If you aren't using them already, you're losing out. In essence, Smart Folders are saved searches that mimic regular folders. This implies that you can quickly access all the files associated with your search without having to navigate through all of Finder's locations.

Here's how to use Smart Folders to organize files on a Mac:

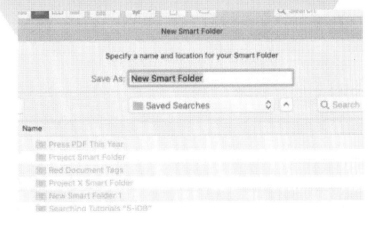

- Press Command + Option to open a new Finder window or choose File > New Smart Folder from the menu.

- You can specify the criteria for your smart folder using the search field that will appear.

- Enter details like the topic, keyword, date, etc., and then pick from the generated suggestions that appear beneath the search.

- By selecting the "+" button next to the Save option, you can add additional search criteria to your search.

- Once finished, click Save and give your Smart folder a name and location.

The fact that Smart Folders don't actually move your files is their best feature. To make it simple for you to locate the related files later, they merely create a reference to them all.

HOW TO ORGANIZE FILES ON MAC DESKTOP

- A disorganized desktop is annoying:
- causes files to be difficult to find.
- takes up RAM, which causes your Mac to run more slowly.

As a result, you should maintain files online in the best possible order.

DECLUTTERING FILES ON YOUR DESKTOP

Sorting them out utilizing your Mac's view options is an effective way to clear your desktop.

Remove all of the icons from your display to start curating your desktop from scratch. Then use Finder to select particular files to be shown by performing the following actions:

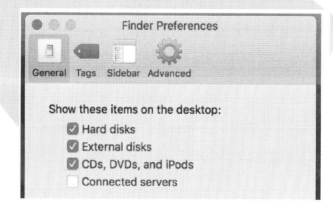

- Choose Finder Preferences from the menu that appears after clicking the Finder icon.

- To select the file types you want on your desktop, go to the General tab.

- If you frequently work with images and videos from SD cards, for instance, you might want to select external disks under "Show these items on the desktop."

Let's say you want to arrange the items that are currently on your desktop. By using the Sort By option, you can see the items that are worth keeping more clearly. Simply select the Sort By option from the View menu on your desktop to sort the files by name, date modified or created, or size.

Using the Clean Up By option, you can decide how to arrange the remaining files after decluttering.

USING STACKS

Try putting your desktop icons in Stacks if you're having trouble condensing them. You can arrange your files into tidy little groups using this macOS feature. To create a stack, simply drag and drop a file on top of another, or click View on your desktop and choose Use Stacks. Then you can organize them based on the dates that they were added, modified, etc.

DESKTOP MINIMALISM

Moving forward, try your best to arrange your desktop in a minimalistic manner. Consider it like this: Only use your desktop for things that require your immediate attention. Only add shortcuts to the apps and files you use frequently so you can access them quickly.

MAC FILE ORGANIZATION USING MAC TAGS

Tags are one of Mac's most underappreciated features. Users can label files with this feature for later quick and simple access. Without moving them, you can group together various files and pieces of media using tags. #Verycool.

The following describes how to tag your files:

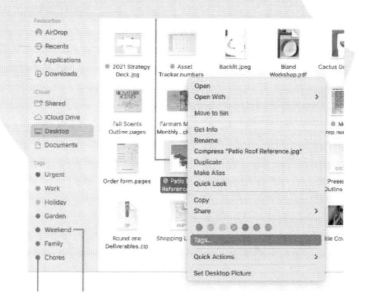

- Select Tags from the shortcut menu that appears when you right-click a file.
- In the box that appears, enter a new tag name or select one of the preexisting tags that are listed.
- Press Return after each tag name to add more tags to the file.
- Pick unique colors for each tag.

After giving files tags, you can keep track of them in the Finder's left sidebar.

Here are some clever tag suggestions:

For workflows:

Active | Archive | Completed

For general/personal matters:

Urgent |To-do | Bills | References | To delete, etc.

SYNCING FILES WITH ICLOUD DRIVE

Last but not least, iCloud Drive can assist you in accessing and updating crucial files if you use multiple devices and are constantly on the go. When syncing files, you can even maintain the same organizational structure that you worked so hard to create!

This is how iCloud Drive functions:

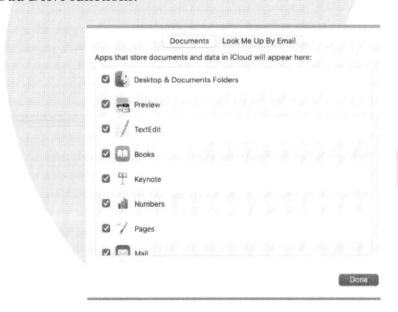

On any current Apple device running the newest OS, iCloud Drive is installed automatically.

- By going to System Preferences, selecting iCloud, and choosing iCloud Drive, Mac users can enable iCloud Drive.

- You can choose which files and folders you want to be synced, but by default, your Desktop and Documents folder will be saved to iCloud.

- All of your devices where iCloud Drive is enabled will be updated with any changes made to those documents.

- Your newly created documents will be kept in iCloud Drive in addition to your preferred locations.

- By logging into your iCloud account on iCloud.com, you can also access the files in your iCloud Drive. This implies that you can access these files from a Windows-based computer.

CHAPTER TWO
MASTERING SECURITY AND PRIVACY

Mac users can be a very lucrative target and are therefore thought to be worth the effort, even though Macs are less likely to be attacked because there are fewer Macs than PCs—in fact, malware on Macs is decreasing. As a result, viruses and malware may target Macs.

In the trial between Apple and Epic, even Apple's head of software Craig Federighi admitted: "Today, we have a level of malware on the Mac that we don't find acceptable." While his intention was to highlight the advantage of requiring iPhone and iPad users to only download apps from the iOS App Store, the key point is that even Apple staff members acknowledge the existence of Mac viruses.

However, Macs are generally safer than PCs. This is due in part to the Unix-based nature of the Mac operating system, which makes it harder to exploit, as well as the fact that Apple has such tight control over the hardware and software. Additionally, Macs are safer due to the numerous security features and protections that have been incorporated into both the Mac and the Mac operating system, making them harder to exploit.

However, that does not imply that you should regard your Mac as impenetrable. Since hackers and viruses have been targeting Macs, Apple has had to take the security features built into macOS seriously in order to protect its users.

Another thing to keep in mind is that Intel processors are not as secure as the M-series chips that Apple began utilizing in November 2020. However, soon after the M1 Mac was released, Silver Sparrow malware was discovered on it.

HOW APPLE PROTECTS YOUR MAC

As you will see later on, Apple protects your Mac in a number of different ways from viruses and malware. Of course, there are additional steps you can take to support these precautions, like running antivirus software or using a VPN to encrypt your traffic. Being cautious and not opening enigmatic emails or clicking on dubious links is also important. However, can you be certain that your parents wouldn't do the same thing? Fortunately, a Mac comes with built-in security measures that should keep even the least tech-savvy users safe. I'll list them here.

SOFTWARE AND SECURITY UPDATES

Keep your Mac software up to date because Apple makes sure that security updates are frequently pushed out to Macs. Apple makes this simple by enabling automatic Mac updates, so you don't even need to do anything. Observe these steps to configure your Mac to automatically check for updates and update software:

- Open System Preferences (System Settings prior to Ventura).
- then select Software Update under General.
- Ensure that Automatic Updates are On. This should ensure that Apple's released software is downloaded to your Mac.

A normal software update will still require you to restart your Mac, but some security updates can be pushed to your Mac and installed as background updates without requiring you to restart.

Make sure that Install Security Responses and System Files is selected in Ventura, or "Install system data files and security updates" in older OSs, to ensure that you receive background updates as soon as Apple releases them.

This is found in Ventura under System Settings > General > Software Update. Select the (i) next to Automatic Updates.

This is found in System Preferences > Software Update > Advanced prior to Ventura.

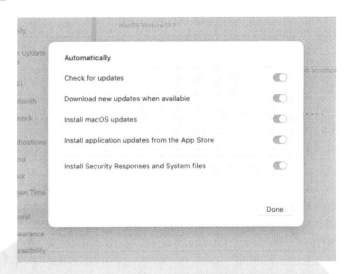

Rapid Security Responses take this a step further by expediting the delivery of security updates for the iPhone, iPad, and Mac. Apple will include the feature in macOS Ventura 13.2 (and iOS 16.3).

Any Rapid Security Responses will be applied immediately when you restart your Mac. By approaching security updates in this manner, Apple is able to release them more quickly and without including them in a larger update.

APP PROTECTIONS

If you want to be completely confident in any app you install, stick to apps from the Mac App Store. Apple has reviewed every app in the Mac App Store, so you can be confident that it will not pose a risk to you. In fact, Apple goes a step further by requiring apps to be transparent about how they use your data, so you can be confident that no of your information will be shared with anyone without your knowledge.

However, even apps not downloaded from the Mac App Store will be checked by Apple before installation - this is the purpose of Gatekeeper, which I mentioned earlier. Gatekeeper verifies that the developer has been verified by Apple and scans the file for malware and malicious code. There may be times when you want to open a Mac app from an unknown developer; in this case, proceed with caution.

Another reason to prefer App Store apps over others is that all apps sold through the Mac App Store must support sandboxing. The sandbox limits apps' access to a Mac's resources and data.

Since the release of macOS 10.15 Catalina in 2019, all Mac apps must be notarized by Apple before they can be launched. Additionally, all Mac apps must now obtain your permission to access your files, whether they are on your Mac, in iCloud Drive, or on external volumes. Before an app can access the camera or microphone, or log what you type, macOS will also ask for your permission.

SAFE SURFING

The above is intended to protect you from malicious apps, but the most serious threats can come from phishing emails, websites, and services you may use online. Safari, Apple's web browser, also provides a variety of online security features. Safari will warn you and prevent you from opening a suspicious website. Every web page is loaded as a separate process in a separate tab, so if there is a problem, you can close that tab without crashing Safari.

Apple also protects Mac users by keeping Flash off Macs. Flash is one of the most common ways for malware to infiltrate computers. Apple discontinued preinstalling Flash with Safari in 2010. As a result, the only way to add Flash was for users to install it themselves, which meant that people became accustomed to living without it. Apple stopped supporting Flash in early 2020, and as of December 31, 2020, even Flash developer Adobe no longer supports Flash. JavaScript also introduces a number of security flaws. JavaScript can be easily disabled in Safari.

- Simply go to Safari > Preferences > Security > and uncheck the box next to Enable JavaScript. It should be noted that if you do this, some visuals on the internet may stop displaying; if this occurs, reapply it.

Apple not only protects your online security, but it also protects your privacy. Apple, for example, employs Intelligent Tracking Prevention to prevent advertisers from tracking users across the web. Users can view a Privacy Report that includes information about all cross-site trackers that Apple has blocked from profiling them.

LOCKDOWN MODE

This is a new layer of security in macOS Ventura that you can use if you are the victim of a cyber attack. You can use it to strengthen your Mac's defenses and set strict limits to prevent the attack from exploiting you.

- To enable it, navigate to System Settings > Privacy & Security > Lockdown Mode, click Turn On next to the Lockdown Mode label, enter your administrator password, and click Turn On & Restart.

When you believe the threat has passed, you can turn off Lockdown Mode and restart.

PASSWORD PROTECTIONS

Apple also monitors your passwords, assisting you in changing them to a more secure option, recommending strong passwords, and even notifying you if Apple suspects your password is involved in a data breach. On that note, Apple also provides iCloud Keychain, a password management system that works across all of your Apple devices, allowing you to log into software and services on any of your devices without remembering individual passwords and log in details. The advantage of this is that you can use strong passwords rather than memorable passwords (which Apple can generate for you). All of your passwords are hidden behind your master password, which is protected by two factor authentication (2FA) for extra security.

Passkeys, which are replacing passwords as an easier and safer way to sign in with macOS Ventura and iOS 16, are another way Apple helps to protect you. Because everything is end-to-end encrypted and there is no password that could be compromised, passkeys are safer. For any website or service, a unique passkey is created and then saved on your device and in your iCloud Keychain so you can access it from other Apple devices. To authenticate, you merely use your Face ID or Touch ID. Although it hasn't yet been widely used because it is new, this should make things safer in the future.

ICLOUD PRIVATE RELAY (ALMOST A VPN)

Because it is a feature of an iCloud+ subscription, iCloud Private Relay isn't accessible to everyone, but it can help you maintain your privacy while using Safari to browse the web. It was included in iOS 15. When Private Relay is turned on, all of your Safari browsing is encrypted and routed through Apple's proxy server, preventing your ISP from seeing what you are doing online.

It's somewhat similar to a VPN but not quite. There are numerous explanations as to why a VPN is preferable. Apple's solution is limited to Safari and does not allow you to conceal your connection's location, which is a major benefit of using a VPN.

- Click on the slider to turn it on.
- Open System Settings
- Click Firewall
- Click Network
- If you want to specify additional security settings click on Options.

POST VENTURA

- In the System Preferences > Security & Privacy pane, select the Firewall tab.
- To access system settings, click the padlock icon in the bottom left corner (you'll be prompted for your login password).

CLICK THE TURN ON FIREWALL BUTTON.

When a dialog box appears, click the Enable Stealth Mode box after clicking the Firewall Options button. This final step makes your computer virtually invisible on open networks, like the free Wi-Fi in a coffee shop.

- To make modifications, select Firewall Options from the Firewall tab. A list of programs and services that can accept inbound connections is provided here.
- Click the "+" next to the list if, for example, when you try to run an app, it displays an error message informing you that it is unable to accept an inbound connection.

It's important to remember that while useful, macOS's Firewall provides only mediocre malware defense. This is because it only protects you from incoming traffic. Its responsibility is to restrict which services and apps can accept incoming connections. It doesn't offer any control over outbound connections, or connections made by apps and services. Therefore, the Firewall on macOS won't prevent malware from connecting to the internet, for instance, if you download it.

So that certain apps can't "phone home" without their knowledge, some people also choose to block outgoing network connections. This also means that malware that was unintentionally installed cannot leak your data without your knowledge.

FILEVAULT

As a way to encrypt your data (and keep it safe in the event that your Mac is stolen or someone gains access to it), Apple provides FileVault. This encryption goes a step further and uses particular hardware to protect your login information if your Mac has an M-series chip.

The settings are located in System Preferences > Security & Privacy (if you are using Ventura) or System Settings > Privacy & Security (if you are using an earlier version of Windows).

Just keep in mind that you'll need to enter your login password or recovery key to access your data, so if you don't have one of these, there's a chance you'll lose it.

FIND MY & ACTIVATION LOCK

Apple also offers additional tools to help you if your Mac is stolen, such as Find My, which lets you track and possibly even find your lost device while also wiping it clean so that your data doesn't end up in the wrong hands. The Activation Lock function of Find My, which allows you to remotely lock your Mac so that only you can use it, is also available on Macs with the T2 chip and M1 Macs.

Another security measure is the fingerprint scanner Touch ID, which is available on some Macs. It can be used for Apple Pay, software and service logins, and Mac unlocking. So, if your Mac is stolen or if someone uses it maliciously, Apple will protect it. Apple also gives you defense against malicious software, control over whether your data is accessible, and protection from misuse. You can use Activation Lock if your Mac has an M-series chip or the T2 security chip, which is found in some Intel Macs, so that if it is lost or stolen, only you will be able to erase and reactivate it.

CHAPTER THREE

TROUBLESHOOTING AND MAINTENANCE

Overall, operating a Mac is a hassle-free process. Daily problems are extremely rare, and many users have no problems using their systems for years. However, because Macs are complex machines, they can experience performance-degrading problems like bugs, erratically behaving apps, and network problems.

Consider your Mac to be a car. Years of neglecting maintenance can cause a car to continue to run fine, but eventually it will catch up with you, leaving you stranded and broken down in the middle of nowhere. Regular maintenance keeps a car in top shape and extends its lifespan by years. The same applies to your Mac. If you take care of it, it will take care of you.

MAC TROUBLESHOOTING

By acting up, I mean that macOS might become sluggish or unresponsive, or that some apps might crash. By using the steps listed below, you can quickly resolve the majority of those problems. When you call or tweet Apple support, they'll probably ask you to go through those steps.

FIX COMMON MAC PROBLEMS

Please be aware that not every issue necessitates going through all of those steps, particularly steps 8 through 10.

- Create a new user account
- Reboot Mac
- Delete Caches folders
- Reset PRAM/NVRAM

- Boot into Safe Mode
- Repair disk permissions
- Reinstall macOS
- Verify disk (and repair if necessary)
- Reset SMC
- Reset Safari and clear caches
- Update to the latest version of macOS

1. REBOOT MAC

Rebooting your computer may be the easiest solution for your problem, depending on it. This is especially true when a specific application is acting inappropriately. The first action I advise taking is a quick reboot of a Mac.

2. RESET PRAM AND NVRAM

How do PRAM and NVRAM work? Source: apple.com

If your Mac is turned off, it still stores some settings in a specific memory location (barring a battery problem, as will be discussed below). This is kept in memory known as NVRAM on Macs with Intel processors and PRAM on Macs with PowerPC processors.

Reset PRAM and NVRAM by following these steps:

- Switch off your computer.
- Switch on the computer.
- Before you hear the startup sound, hold down the Command-Option-P-R keys while pressing them.
- Keep pressing the keys until the computer restarts and the startup sound appears a second time.
- Let go of the keys.

3. BOOT INTO SAFE MODE

When your Mac restarts, press and hold the shift key until you see a progress bar at the bottom of the screen to enter Safe Mode. That means your Mac is starting up in Safe Mode, which clears out a few extra caches. Reboot normally after entering Safe Mode without pressing the Shift key.

4. RESET THE SYSTEM MANAGEMENT CONTROLLER (SMC)

Depending on whether you're using a desktop (such as an iMac or Mac Mini) or a MacBook, different steps are needed to reset the SMC. The steps for both platforms are listed below:

HOW TO RESET A DESKTOP'S SMC

- Shut off your Mac.
- Remove the power plug.
- Take 15 seconds to wait.
- Reconnect the power cord.
- To turn on your Mac, hold down the power button for five seconds.
- How to Reset a MacBook's SMC Non-Removable Battery
- Put your MacBook to sleep.
- Remove the MacBook's MagSafe or USB-C power adapter.
- Press Shift-Control-Option on the left side of the built-in keyboard while simultaneously pressing the power button. Hold the power button and these keys in place for 10 seconds.* Turn off all the keys.
- Reattach the power cord.
- To restart your Mac, press the power button once more.

5. REPAIR DISK PERMISSIONS

Since OS X El Capitan automatically protects file system permissions, fixing disk permissions has become obsolete. Please keep reading if you are still using OS X Yosemite or an earlier version. Even if your Mac is operating without any problems, you should occasionally repair the disk permissions.

To do this, launch Disk Utility (depending on your OS X version, it will be in Launchpad; alternatively, you can press Command + Space and type Disk Utility to open it via Spotlight), choose your main hard drive (i.e., Macintosh HD), and then select "Repair Disk Permissions."

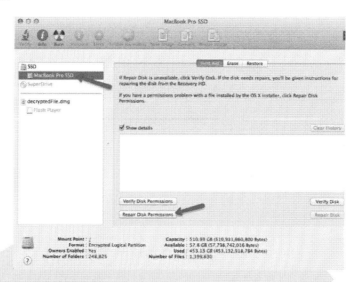

6. VERIFY AND REPAIR DISK

Disk Utility allows you to check the disk's and file system's integrity. Apple refers to that function as "First Aid" in more recent iterations of macOS.

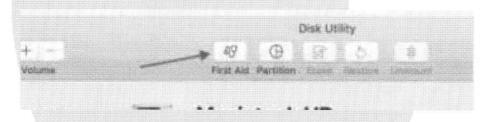

It shouldn't typically find anything wrong, but if it does, you must fix it. You must first boot into the so-called Recovery Mode to accomplish this. Restart your Mac while holding down the Command + R keys until the Apple logo appears to enter Recovery Mode.

Once you're in the recovery console, open Disk Utility, choose your computer's primary hard drive, and then, depending on your version of macOS/OS X, select Repair Disk or First Aid.

7. RESET SAFARI AND CLEAR CACHES

Note: On more recent macOS versions, there is no longer a reset option for Safari.

Launch Safari and choose "Reset Safari..." from the menu in the upper left corner of the screen after clicking on Safari to clear all of its caches. On an older version, you might need to go to Preferences to clear all caches because I'm using Safari 6.

You might want to uncheck "Remove saved names and passwords" or create a backup copy of your passwords before clearing everything out, depending on whether you use a separate password manager (like 1Password).

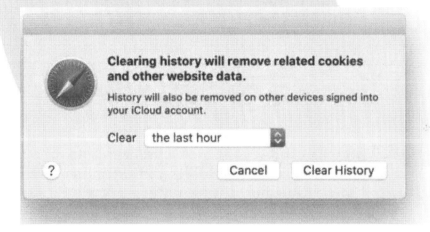

You can still clear all Safari caches on more recent versions of macOS by selecting Safari > Clear History. An alternative is to use Safari > Preferences > Privacy > Manage Website Data to delete website data from specific web pages.

8. CREATE A NEW USER ACCOUNT

Rarely, issues with your user profile may arise, in which case setting up a new user account is the best course of action. You might lose settings and preferences, so it is obvious that this is an intrusive step. As a result, I view this as almost the last option. However, it's important to note that I frequently employ this method to determine whether a problem pertains to my user account or not. There is no need to go through the hassle of adding a new user if it is not.

Open System Preferences and select Users & Groups to add a new user account. Then click the plus sign after clicking the lock icon at the bottom of the screen. To create your new account, adhere to the instructions on the screen.

ROUTINE MAC MAINTENANCE TIPS TO PREVENT YOUR SYSTEM FROM RUNNING INTO TROUBLE

LEARN HOW TO BACK UP YOUR DATA

Always make backing up your data a top priority. Even Macs are not impenetrable. All of your hard work and priceless photos are lost forever if something goes horribly wrong and you don't have a backup plan in place.

But enough with the macabre content. All of your files are routinely backed up to an external storage device by Mac's built-in Time Machine so they can be easily restored.

You must attach an external hard drive to your MacBook or iMac in order to set up Time Machine. After that, scheduling backups is simple:

- Select System Settings > General > Time Machine from the Apple menu.
- Select Disk by clicking.
- Click Use Disk after selecting your disk from the list. If Time Machine has not yet been configured on your Mac, you may need to click Add Backup Disk and adhere to the on-screen instructions.

Following that, Time Machine will begin creating hourly backups for the previous 24 hours, daily backups for the previous month, and weekly backups for all prior months. By opening the window for the item, items can be recovered from the Time Machine. Open the Mail app, for instance, if you unintentionally deleted an email. To find the necessary item, click the Time Machine icon (the tiny clock icon) and then navigate through the timeline.

CLEAN UP JUNK FILES

Use Mac's Optimized Storage feature if you're using a newer version of macOS. It automatically cleans out Trash, minimizes clutter, improves storage by deleting previously watched movies and TV shows, and transfers some files to iCloud.

Aim to always have at least 10% of your disk space free for optimum performance. You can achieve this by routinely purging unnecessary files from your computer.

- Open the main Apple menu > Settings > General > Storage.
- Go to the colored bar and select Recommendations.

Here, you can find junk in a variety of categories quickly. Choose Applications and sort them by Last Accessed for a quick start.

Both will assist you in quickly clearing out space, but neither provides a thorough cleanup. All you are actually doing when you move an item to the Trash is moving the main app or item file. Other related garbage, such as cache and preference files, are overlooked and take up space on your disk.

REMOVE THOSE MYRIADS OF DESKTOP ICONS

Mac must contribute RAM for each app, file, or screenshot on your desktop. Therefore, it uses more system resources the more things you have on there. Use CleanMyMac X to remove anything you don't need from your desktop and group items into folders to keep it clutter-free.

UTILIZE THE STACKS FUNCTION.

Mac OS Catalina is where this started. Stacks, a basic feature for organizing things.

- On your desktop, right-click a blank area.
- Tap Use Stacks.

CHAPTER FOUR
OPTIMIZING PRODUCTIVITY

Many of us carefully design our home offices to support productive and comfortable work—I know I spent hours selecting my desk surface, rug, and other accents. We frequently overlook giving our computers the same attention during this process. Your Mac serves as the portal through which you complete all of your work, making it just as much of a "office space" as your actual workspace. As such, you should make an effort to configure and optimize it for productivity.

I learned as a professional musician not to practice too much while staring in the mirror because it consumes too much "brain juice" because our brains expend a lot of energy processing visual data. What really matters—my ability to judge the sound I'm producing on my instrument—is diminished when I watch myself play.

Similar to this, computers frequently show us pointless visuals. Because we don't require as much visual feedback as other types of workers, we can eliminate obtrusive interface elements and screen clutter.

Here, I'll recommend a few applications to fill in the gaps in native macOS functionality as well as some unusual, minimalist tweaks to speed up your workflow.

1. USE THE FOCUS FEATURE

Focus is a feature that lets you filter your notifications in macOS Mojave. Only my Zapier coworkers and emergency contacts are permitted to contact me during work hours thanks to a focus I set up for that purpose. Additionally, I've set up Focuses (Foci?) for sleeping, exercising, and practicing music.

For those of us who own an iPhone, Focuses configured on your Mac will be automatically mirrored on mobile, controlling your phone's notifications. This native feature is the one I call out first because it has greatly improved my ability to focus. It's wonderful to see Apple taking our attention spans into account.

2. CREATE SEPARATE USERS

Consider setting up distinct user accounts for computing at home and at work. To keep things separate, you can, for example, only sign into Slack with your work user and only sign into Messages with your personal user. Make sure to configure a unique fingerprint for each user in System Preferences > Touch ID to enable quick switching.

3. USE KEYBOARD SHORTCUTS

The repeated motion of moving your hand from your keyboard to your mouse and back results in a small but measurable time-loss, making mice and trackpads less efficient input devices.

I use Zendesk shortcuts all day long as a Customer Champion at Zapier to keep my fingers on the home row and my attention on our customers rather than my computer. For Zoom, Gmail, and probably every other app you use, there are keyboard shortcuts. You can even make your own shortcuts, or use a program like Keyboard Maestro to advance.

You can actually switch the caps lock and command keys on your Mac's keyboard under System Preferences > Keyboard > Modifier Keys if your pinky starts to get sore from repeatedly pressing the command key.

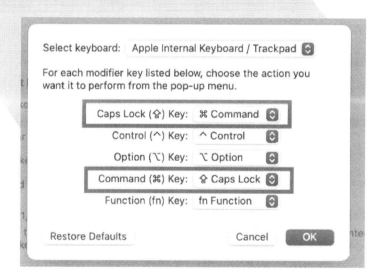

4. CLEAN UP YOUR DESKTOP

Think about never using your desktop. A long-standing multitasking issue has an imperfect solution in desktop environments (more on this later). I therefore advise against using folders or icons on your desktop. This is why:

Your desktop will be less visually cluttered overall if there are no icons there.

You'll have to use your home folder wisely and actively sort files if you don't have icons on your desktop.

Applications don't have to compete for screen space on your desktop if there aren't any icons there.

Use a Finder window instead if you need to drag and drop files, say, into an email or from a web page to save.

While you're at it, experiment with a desktop background that isn't a wallpaper. It isn't visually distracting, for starters. But it also serves as a reminder to myself that I am here to create, not to consume when I am in front of my computer and have a blank page in front of me. Beautiful images and videos can wait until after work.

5. DON'T USE DOCK

If you don't use Alfred, think of this as a shameless advertisement. I use it for snippets, password retrieval, and countless other purposes. The ability of Alfred to launch apps instantly by invoking your keyboard shortcut and typing the app's name is a simple but frequently disregarded feature. If that sounds like a lot of work, try it out and keep in mind how much space the macOS Dock takes up on the screen, how long it takes for it to reappear after being hidden, and how much time you spend using the mouse to search for apps.

- Simply hiding your Dock, please: Dock & Menu Bar > System Preferences Dock should be automatically hidden and shown.

Another excellent free app that lets you disable some unnecessary visual components in macOS is TinkerTool. Consider disabling automations for the Dock and Launchpad in particular. You'll be surprised at how much more responsive these elements are once these are disabled, should you need to access them right away.

6. REMOVE MENU BAR AND TOOLBAR ICONS

Numerous native macOS apps have toolbars with resizable icon sets. These icons, in particular in Finder and Apple Mail, can take up a lot of room. Consider removing all of the toolbar's icons to disable them completely, or at the very least, replace the icons with clickable text. In addition to clearing up the visual environment, this will promote the use of keyboard shortcuts.

I manage the icons in my menu bar using Bartender. I particularly like the Show for Updates feature, which lets you restrict when menu bar icons are displayed. I've set the following criteria:

- Only when the battery is less than 40% charged will the battery icon appear.
- When not connected to a Wi-Fi network, only display the Wi-Fi icon.
- Only display the VPN icon when not connected to a VPN.
- In general, only display the information in your Mac's menu bar that is absolutely necessary to see at all times. To go further, you can always click into Bartender.

7. MANAGE YOUR WINDOWS

It's simple to get lost in a sea of open apps and overlapping windows in this age of multiple monitors and ultrawides. I've had to reconsider how I screen properties while working because I now realize how terrible we are at multitasking.

Here, I'll make a few radical suggestions, with window management being perhaps the most important. Many of us use programs like Magnet or BetterSnapTool to quickly snap or split windows. These are both excellent, but the user must choose how to arrange the windows on the monitor. Try using a tiling window manager if, like me, you prefer to use no more than two or three apps at once. I use Amethyst on the Mac. Here are its actions:

An app's window on my desktop is automatically maximized for full-screen use when it is launched. Not to be confused with a Mac app running in "full screen" mode, which causes the app to disappear from your desktop.

A vertical split is introduced when another app is launched, and your apps are automatically resized so that each takes up half of your screen from left to right. This is especially effective with ultrawide monitors with a 21:9 aspect ratio because splitting the screen vertically creates two spaces with a 4:3 aspect ratio, which is a very comfortable size for using web apps.

The right side of the screen is split horizontally when a third app is started. Currently, the third app occupies the right side of my screen's bottom half. The splits are automatically adjusted and the remaining apps are automatically resized to fill the empty space if any app is closed.

You won't ever need to look for overlapping windows using Mission Control again if you use this method. Amethyst even lets you create exceptions, allowing you to quickly launch System Preferences to make a change if necessary while still allowing apps that only need a small window to float.

But my window management process is more complex than that. I set up the necessary keybindings in System Preferences > Keyboard > Shortcuts > Mission Control to quickly switch between the six static desktops I've added to Mission Control:

choice #1: Go to the desktop

choice #2: Go to desktop 2

choice #3: Change to desktop 3 (and so on).

(Tip: To switch between tabs quickly in Chrome, press command + the tab number. This, along with the keybindings mentioned above, offers a super quick way to navigate desktops and browser tabs on your Mac without ever using the mouse.)

Bindings are among Amethyst's preferences so that focused apps can be quickly moved between desktops.

Shift + Option + desktop number> is how I operate.

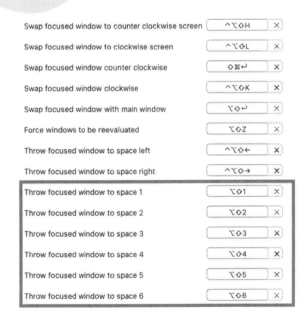

I also use a useful program called SpaceId, which displays the desktop I'm currently using in my menu bar.

By managing my windows in this way with Amethyst, I have completely changed how I use my computer and have prevented countless mouse clicks. As an added benefit, I no longer experience any productivity loss when I don't have my ultrawide monitor with me. Since I always have alternative desktops available to quickly switch to, working on my 13" MacBook Pro screen isn't any less comfortable as a result.

My desktops might look like this on an average workday:

- When using my ultrawide monitor, Chrome splits into two windows on my first desktop.
- Desktop 2: To use a second Chrome window for customer service
- Computer 3: Slack
- Apple Music on computer #4
- Emacs (note-taking, to-do lists, and development learning) on desktop 5
- Firefox and Messages (personal apps) on desktop 6

8. CLEAN UP YOUR BROWSER

For all work-related tasks, I use Chrome, while for personal browsing, I use Firefox. I like being able to divide up my browsing because I don't want my history, bookmarks, or logged-in accounts to conflict with each other. Choosy is a fantastic app that lets you select which browser opens in specific circumstances. Here are some of the criteria I have set under System Preferences > General with Choosy as my default browser (as opposed to Chrome or Firefox):

- When clicking a link in Slack, always open it in Chrome.
- When clicking a link in Messages, always open it in Firefox.
- When opening a URL from Alfred, ask me which browser to open.

(And before you ask, yep, Choosy also works with Chrome profiles.)

In Chrome, I'd also advise eliminating the search suggestions. Like me, you probably keep a ton of bookmarks organized. However, sometimes it might be difficult to locate the correct bookmark while using the URL bar. If you want Chrome to only propose URLs linked to your bookmarks when you enter "dashboard," for example, rather than images of automobile dashboards, you might want to disable Chrome's "Autocomplete searches and URLs" option:

> Chrome > Settings > Sync and Google services > Autocomplete searches and URLs.

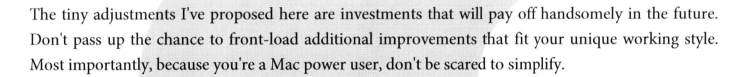

Autocomplete searches and URLs
Sends some cookies and searches from the address bar and search box to your default search engine

The tiny adjustments I've proposed here are investments that will pay off handsomely in the future. Don't pass up the chance to front-load additional improvements that fit your unique working style. Most importantly, because you're a Mac power user, don't be scared to simplify.

CHAPTER FIVE

EXPLORING MAC APPS AND SERVICES

Y ou might or might not have noticed that macOS has a menu item for programs named Services. The ability to access a feature from one app without opening it is provided via services. In essence, therefore, it's a technique to get to shortcuts that will let you do brief jobs. You may either build your own shortcuts or utilize the ones that are already included in the Services menu.

HOW TO USE SERVICES

First, to find Services:

You may utilize the Services menu at various times, and there are a variety of alternatives accessible.

For instance, open Safari and pick some text.

Select Safari from the menu at the top, then scroll down to Services.

Here, a wide range of possibilities are visible. Depending on the applications you've installed and whether you've modified your Services menu, some of the choices might not be visible.

Right-clicking on the phrases you marked will also take you to the services menu.

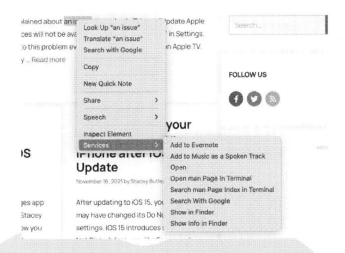

When you choose files, further Services are offered. To find out what you can do with the chosen files, either pick them on your desktop or in Finder, then click Finder from the top menu, scroll down to Services.

HOW TO CUSTOMIZE YOUR SERVICES MENU

You can customize your Services menu in System Preferences. You can:

- Select and deselect the already displayed Service menu items.
- Make keyboard shortcuts for the things you use frequently.
- Using Automator, add new Service menu items.

Some of the items in the Services menu choices aren't applicable to a certain app. If you can't utilize certain items, they won't appear in the Services menu of the app.

SELECT/UNSELECT MENU ITEMS

- Go to Apple menu > System Preferences. Click on Keyboard, then click on the Shortcuts tab.
- Select Services from the menu on the window's left.
- The whole Service menu will be displayed. Scroll down to see more.
- Select the checkbox next to an option to add it. Remove it by unticking the box.
- Under a category, such as Pictures, Messaging, and Development, each of the choices is listed. If you click the "carrots" next to the category headers to collapse that category, you may navigate through the alternatives more easily.

ADD KEYBOARD SHORTCUTS FOR SERVICES

You may program a keyboard shortcut for any Services menu choice that you know you'll use frequently. You won't have to go through the menu every time you want to utilize the service thanks to this.

- Services are highlighted in the left-side list under Shortcuts in System Preferences > Keyboard > Shortcuts.

> Select a menu item for Services. "Add Shortcut" ought to display next to the item. Add Shortcut by selecting it.
>
> The keystrokes you wish to utilize for your keyboard shortcut should be typed.
>
> After you type your shortcut, "Add Shortcut" could reappear. Your shortcut key combination will display next to the item when you click Add Shortcut or another item in the list.

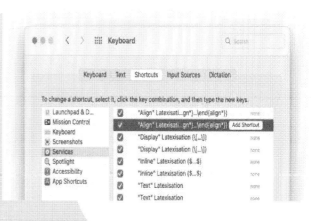

CREATE NEW ITEMS USING AUTOMATOR

There are a ton of tutorials online for utilizing Automator, as well as tons of suggestions for making things that would speed up your productivity. You may create an Automation to change the kind of files, shut down all of your open programs, or rename a group of files in a meaningful way without altering them one by one.

ESSENTIAL MAC APPS

The well-known Mac programs like Evernote, 1Password, Dropbox, Skype, OneNote, or Google Drive aren't included in our list of important Mac apps since they tend to be less well-known. Additionally, Big Sur and Catalina, the most recent macOS versions, are also compatible with every software on this page.

Let's get going.

- Raycast is a potent Spotlight substitute for the Mac that enables rapid program searches, online searches, and more. With JavaScript, you can also design unique processes.

- Consider Notion to be a note-taking program that also doubles as a wiki, to-do list organizer, calendar, spreadsheet, and project management tool.

- You no longer need a Microsoft 365 subscription or Office license to use Outlook, which is the greatest email software for Mac. A suitable substitute for Apple Mail is Spark.

- Magnet is the ideal Mac window management application, allowing you to drag and drop windows and resize them using customisable keyboard shortcuts. Additionally, windows may be moved among several monitors. Rectangle is still another selection.

- Setapp - a bundled set of high-end Mac utilities and applications. Favorites like Capto for screen recording and CleanshotX for screen capture are included.

- Shottr - A creative screenshot tool for Mac that makes it simple to take and annotate screenshots. Both OCR and full web page capture are possible. I also utilize Xnapper and CleanShot X.

- ImageOptim - Before adding any photos to your website, make sure to run them via ImageOptim. Your image files' size will be decreased by the program without sacrificing visual quality.

- Warp - a contemporary Mac Terminal substitute. It is quick, gorgeous, and has AI search to translate spoken words into shell commands that can be executed.

- Site Sucker - Save whole websites, including their graphics and PDF files, on your local drive so you can browse them offline. wget-like, but with a graphical user interface.

- App Cleaner - The best Mac uninstaller will automatically erase all the superfluous files that a software leaves behind on the disk.

- Maccy - a clipboard manager that allows you to paste copied text into other programs with a single shortcut and keeps whatever you copy to the clipboard. [CopyClip] is a respectable substitute.

- Clean Me - Delete all the system logs, cache, and temporary files that your Mac can simply get rid of to free up space on your computer.

- Dozer - a great substitute for the well-known Bartender app. The app icons that display on the Mac menu bar may be swiftly rearranged or even hidden.

CHAPTER SIX
CUSTOMIZATION AND PERSONALIZATION

t's simple to change the background, interface colors, icons, audio, etc. using macOS. Customize your profile picture, the Dock, the notification sound, and other options that affect how the system operates to make your Mac seem like it is truly yours.

Additionally, you may use third-party tools to perform more extensive customizations, alter the appearance of programs in Dark Mode, and establish custom Finder window backgrounds. I'll show you some methods to personalize your Mac in the sections below.

Apple has shifted to a user interface that is simpler with time. MacOS functions satisfactorily out of the box, although it may be improved. Making a few settings your own will improve how well macOS functions for you.

You may easily alter the appearance and feel of your Mac. Learn how to personalize your Mac by modifying your macOS options to suit your preferences.

PERSONALISE THE APPEARANCE ON YOUR MAC

It's beneficial to customize a Mac and make it uniquely yours. Even entire websites exist that are devoted to Mac theming. I'll show you what Apple has to offer rather than using third-party tools for various appearances.

I'll be utilizing the most recent operating system, macOS 10.12 Sierra, for this lesson. Whatever version you are using, you'll discover that the fundamental ideas are the same, but with minor variations. Let's now experiment with some fun methods to modify your Mac's aesthetic setup.

1. HAVE THE WALLPAPER CHANGE ON ITS OWN EVERY FEW HOURS OR DAYS.

I've always had trouble with the idea of using desktop wallpaper as a metaphor for computers. I assume it doesn't feel the same to change the tablecloth.

- Go to System Preferences > Desktop & Screen Saver to alter the wallpaper (or tablecloth). Use the Apple icon in the upper left of the menu bar to get there, or press Command-Space to open Spotlight and type "Desktop" to discover the option.

- You may choose to have the wallpaper automatically change when you've chosen a picture for it. The frequency at which the wallpaper changes may also be configured. Put a check in the Change Picture: box by clicking the tick box, then choose the desired interval from the drop-down option.

- You may choose to have the background photos appear at random if you'd like. Toggle the Random order box to the on position by clicking the check box.

- Use a designated folder in iPhoto to store the wallpaper pictures in order to keep everything organized. You don't need to worry about adding one when you download something new since the Desktop & Screen Saver window constantly keeps them current.

As an alternative, you may utilize any Mac folder as long as it contains many images.

2. TURN ON SCREEN SAVERS AND OTHER DEVICES WITH HOT CORNERS.

- Click on the Screen Saver tab in the Desktop & Screen Saver settings window to browse available screen savers. There is a Hot Corners button in the bottom right corner.

- With the help of the macOS system feature known as Hot Corners, you may perform predefined tasks by clicking on any of the four corners of the screen. It could do something different, like open LaunchPad or the Notification Center, or it might start a screen saver.

- To activate a feature, move the mouse pointer to the designated corner.

3. ADD SPACERS TO THE DOCK

Your Mac's dock can quickly grow crowded with several program icons. If so, separating the symbols with a space may assist make more sense of the situation.

The spacers that this command creates are transparent tiles that may be quickly removed from the dock if necessary.

- defaults write com.apple.dock persistent-apps -array-add '{"tile-type"="spacer-tile";}'; killall Dock

Open Terminal and type the following command to activate a blank tile:

The dock will temporarily vanish after the instruction has been carried out and reload with an invisible tile to make a gap.

The invisible tile may be moved along the dock to provide a space between icons as needed, or it can be removed if it is no longer needed.

4. MODIFY THE MAC OPERATING SYSTEM'S COLOR SCHEME

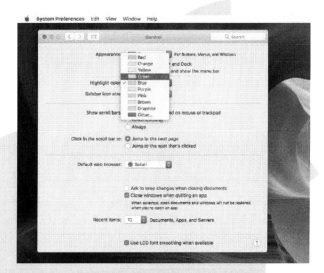

- Open System Preferences > General and adjust the Highlight Color: setting to a different color if you'd rather have anything other than the usual blue for highlighted text.
- You may choose any color from the colour picker using the Other... option in addition to the eight options in the menu.

There is another appearance choice here called Graphite, which makes all app windows, menus, and buttons more monochromatic. There are just two colors available: blue and graphite, so if you like a very plain appearance without the vibrant close, minimize, and zoom buttons on the window bars, this is for you.

5. ADD DOCK MAGNIFICATION, HIDE IT, AND CHANGE ITS POSITION

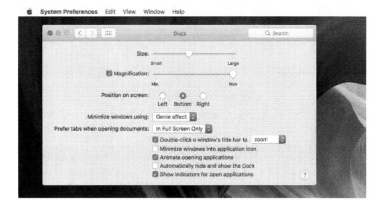

The Mac's dock does not immediately catch your eye out of the box like it could on previous Macs. This is as a result of magnification being disabled.

- To use it, click the Apple icon in the menu bar's upper left corner, choose Dock, and then click Turn Magnification On.

You may choose to conceal the dock from this menu as well, which is helpful to maximize screen space, particularly on tiny laptop screens. By moving the mouse to the area of the screen where the dock is located while concealed, you may reveal it.

The dock may be moved and positioned on either the left or right side of the screen. If you move the dock to the sides, it will also seem differently; it will be more two-dimensional and resemble OS X 10.4 Tiger.

HOW TO CUSTOMISE THE MENU BAR ON YOUR MAC

The menu bar isn't typically utilized to its full potential. There are some incredibly inventive things you can do with the information there, but other apps utilize it for more information. Let's have a look at some great Mac Menu Bar customization options.

ADD SECONDS AND A DATE TO THE TIME

On the menu bar, you may show more than simply the time. To expand, click the time now and choose Open Date & Time Preferences. A place to set the date and time may be found on the main tab.

Go straight to the Clock tab if that is accurate. Analogize the time instead of Digital showing the time in seconds the time separators flash, Use a clock with a 24-hour cycle, reveal or conceal the AM/PM markers, Display the weekday, Display the current date in the menu bar and announce the time every quarter, half, and hour.

Mac OS hides a ton of fascinating time-related features. The date being shown in the menu bar is important, and seconds might be useful if you want to be on time. Remember that the Language & Text window allows you to modify the date format. I'll expand on that later.

ADD BATTERY PERCENTAGE AND LIFE TIME

If your portable Mac's battery indicator is only an icon in the menu bar, you need to update it so you can view additional information. Click it once it is plugged in, then choose Show Percentage to receive a reading charge. Then test the situation by unplugging the MacBook's charging adapter.

Note: In Mountain Lion, the option to display the battery's remaining life in the present mode was eliminated. Click the battery icon and check for that choice if you're running an earlier OS X version.

HOW TO SET PERSONAL PREFERENCES ON A MAC

Everyone enjoys adjusting things to fit their own settings. The fun tiny settings your Mac allows you to make are in this area.

CHANGING THE ACTION ON INSERTING A CD OR DVD

If your Mac even has a drive for video discs, you might not always want DVD Player to start up when you put a disc in there.

Open the CDs & DVDs tab in System Preferences to modify the behavior. If there is a function you want to change, click it and choose "Open other application..." Select Ignore if you want to completely disable the functionality.

If you have a custom function, you can even use Run Script.

ADJUST WHAT SPOTLIGHT SEARCHES AND HOW IT'S ORDERED

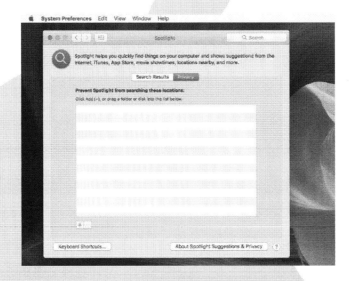

Maybe you have some private files that shouldn't be included in the search results. If so, you may remove them from a Spotlight query for the whole system. This is how:

- Launch System Preferences and click Spotlight
- Click the Privacy tab
- Click the + button to add a folder or entire disc you don't want to be displayed.

Additionally, you may change how Spotlight presents the search results. Deselect the categories you don't want to view in the Search Results page, or move them into the order you desire. You may also modify the Spotlight shortcut here.

CHANGE THE DEFAULT DICTIONARY ON YOUR MAC

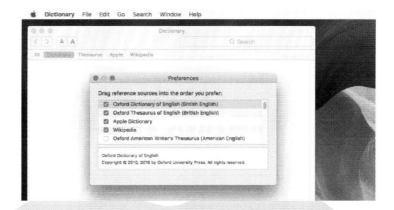

One of the most helpful applications on the Mac is the Dictionary app from Apple. It's easy to use and effective.

However, if you're anything like me, you prefer to look up terms in the British dictionary, which is a genuine English dictionary. Go to the Preferences window and tick the box for the language you want to be shown in the app's main window to enable a different language.

Two of the 10 dictionaries and thesauruses that come with the Mac—the Apple one and Wikipedia—are more resources than dictionaries.

CHANGE APP ICONS ON YOUR MAC

Even the app icons on your Mac may be changed if you're truly into personalizing and making things your own. Although there are tools for this, changing an app's icon manually on a Mac is a very simple task.

- Find an icon online and download it. The next step won't be a problem if the file is a typical.icns file.

- Choose the.png or.jpeg icon and launch Preview to examine the file. To replicate the selection, pick All in the Edit menu. Because they don't always have transparent backgrounds, regular.png files don't function.

- Locate the app you want to change, choose it, and then click Get Info. You may also use the Command-I keyboard shortcut.

- Click the small icon in the top left corner of the app and Command-V to paste the new icon.

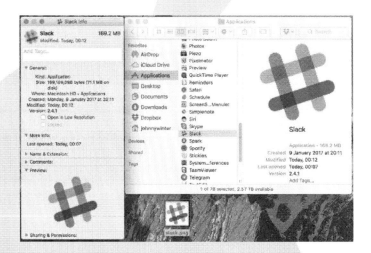

- Select the little custom icon in the Get Info box and hit the Delete key on your keyboard to erase it.

manually: While most programs respond well to this method, Apple's own apps could not.

MAKE FINDER OPEN IN A DIFFERENT FOLDER THAN ALL MY FILES

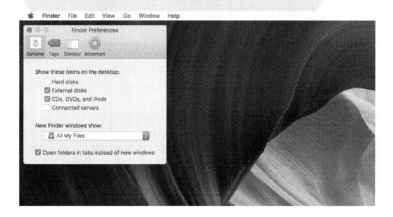

When you open Finder on new Macs, the All My Files directory is shown by default.

Personally, I find that objectionable. Thankfully, there is a method to alter it.

- Select the General tab in Finder's Preferences.

- From the drop-down option underneath the New Finder windows, select a folder.

- Use any folder on your hard disk by selecting Other.

SET REGIONAL VARIATIONS ON YOUR MAC

The date format is different in the United States than it is in the rest of the globe. Consider altering the format to one that makes logical sense, such as ascending DD-MM-YYYY or descending YYYY-MM-DD. An ISO standard governs the latter. For instance, spreadsheets in the ISO format may be appropriately sorted.

- The date need not be formatted in the same way as the rest of the USA. The Language & Text pane of System Preferences allows you to customize that and other features. Click the Region tab when you get there. Here are some options for you:

- Make the Week Begin on Any Day - Maybe you'd want the week to begin on Monday. Select the day to start the week by selecting it from the drop-down menu next to First day of the week.

- Change the date format by selecting Customize next to the Dates section and rearranging the items as needed. You may drag and drop the values and arrange them whatever you like because Apple made everything really simple. Even the era, AD, might be included if desired.

- Change the time format to reflect the inclusion of milliseconds. In the Times section's Customize screen, Apple offers you a selection. Once more, it's a drag-and-drop operation.

- Change the decimal characters and currency separators. Some people prefer that the decimal characters be commas and commas points. If that describes you, modify things up by clicking Customize underneath the Numbers section. The values can be changed to any character.

- Change Your Currency or Measurement Unit: You have options for your current currency and measurement units. Although there are several currencies, only the UK, US, or metric measuring systems are available. Because it employs both imperial and metric measures, the UK is uncommon in this regard.

HOW TO CUSTOMISE YOUR MAC FINDER

You should claim the macOS file browser as your own. Let's examine how to personalize it and the fun features your Mac Finder offers.

ORGANISE YOUR FOLDERS AUTOMATICALLY

Having a folder totally altered by improper organization is irritating. The toolbar in Finder contains options for these kind of items.

- Select the organizational strategy that best suits you by clicking the button that resembles a tiny selection of icons as seen in the screen photo above. The greatest thing to utilize is name since it always appears in place.

- However, you can do anything, including Kind, Size, and Label. Alternately, move objects off the grid to somewhat muck them up.

REMOVE MOUNTED DISCS FROM THE DESKTOP

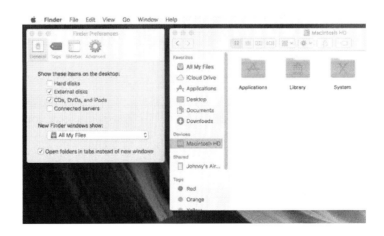

You might not want the CD or an external hard drive to take up space on your desktop.

> Open Finder's Preferences and choose the General tab. Deselect one of the Show these things on the desktop choices.

That will clear off some clutter on the desktop.

BRING BACK THE STATUS BAR

The size of a selection, the number of files in a folder, and other relevant information used to be displayed in a status bar at the bottom of the Finder pane.

In OS X 10.7 Lion, it was disabled by default, but you can always restore it using the simple keyboard shortcut Command / (Command Oblique).

As an alternative, choose Show Status Bar from the View menu.

CHAPTER SEVEN

ENHANCING MULTIMEDIA EXPERIENCE

Today, video chats are a crucial element of life in the post-lockdown era. They are used by businesses for meetings, by societies for planning, and by family members for catch-up. A high-quality video conference may ease this requirement and enhance your overall conversation.

Although macOS's volume and sound settings are simple and intuitive, some users might like more control over their Mac's audio.

However, some individuals might not have a positive experience while using their Macs for video calling. You may occasionally resolve the problems that could degrade the quality of your video calls on your own. Therefore, I've compiled a list of improvements you should consider to enhance the audio and visual quality of your calls.

ADJUST THE SETTINGS FOR VIDEO CALLING APPS

Many developers work to make sure their video call applications can lower call quality as necessary because many of the apps we use cater to a wide variety of users with varied levels of internet stability. While this is a positive thing, if any of these aspects have a negative impact on you, it could start to bother you. I've listed a few well-known applications along with suggestions for how to make calls on them sound better.

FACETIME

FaceTime, however, doesn't provide as many settings for customization as other programs. There are several options you may enable, nevertheless, that might improve your display.

If you have a Mac with Apple silicon, one of these capabilities is Portrait mode, which is featured in macOS Monterey (and subsequent versions). This setting distorts your surroundings so that all eyes are on you, enhancing your face.

To activate Portrait mode, adhere to following steps:

- Open the Control Center from the menu bar while on a video conversation in the FaceTime app.
- Select Portrait under Video Effects in the upper left corner.
- By selecting it one more with the Portrait button, you may deselect it.

USE AN EXTERNAL WEBCAM

If you want cutting-edge movies for your video conversations, a MacBook may not be sufficient, especially if you use a MacBook Air, which is only equipped with a 720p camera (with the exception of the 2022 model with the M2 CPU).

This issue can be resolved since an external camera is always preferable than a built-in one because they are often larger and contain better circuitry. You may improve your video quality by purchasing a nice 1080p camera for about $100.

Don't forget to adjust the app's settings so you can utilize the camera after connecting your external device.

USE YOUR IPHONE AS A WEBCAM

You can use the Continuity Camera feature if your Mac is running macOS Ventura or later and your iPhone is running iOS 16 or later. The main camera on your iPhone may quickly take the place of the webcam on your Mac.

It's cool that Continuity Camera eliminates the need for an additional external webcam. Additionally, the iPhone's camera is of higher quality than most webcams. Additionally, it is wireless and has a variety of distinctive capabilities, such as Desk View, which lets you simultaneously display your face and the contents of your desk.

TURN OFF THE AUDIO VOLUME POPS

The popping noise that is played each time the volume control buttons on the keyboard are pushed is likely familiar to many Mac users. Not everyone likes to hear this indication, which is designed to show how loud or quiet the system audio will be if left at the recently chosen level.

If you wish to permanently disable pops, you may do so in the macOS settings menus by choosing the Sound Preferences... option after choosing the volume control in the menu bar. Alternately, choose System Preferences, Sound, and the Apple logo from the menu bar.

Uncheck the box next to the option labeled Play feedback when volume is modified under the Sound Effects tab.

In the event that it is desirable for the audio confirmation to remain active, there is also a temporary method to turn off the pop sound effect. The popping sounds can be muted by hitting the volume adjustment keys on the keyboard while holding down the Shift key; the popping sounds resume when the key is released.

FINER VOLUME ADJUSTMENTS

The volume keys on the keyboard are arguably the most often utilized method for adjusting the sound level. This approach only allows for 16 alternative sound output settings (or 17, if you count quiet), and there are occasions when you wish to reach a volume that is halfway between the two.

If the icon in the menu bar is enabled in the Sound options, the obvious method to achieve this is to alter the volume using it. If it isn't included in the menu, you may quickly adjust the volume using the keyboard's volume control buttons while simultaneously holding down Option-Shift.

The number of volume settings increases to 64 when this key combination is used, in addition to mute, and the volume control buttons now modify the volume level in quarter-step increments. It should be noted that tapping the volume keys without using the additional modifier keys will automatically increase the volume to the next full step if the volume is set to a quarter- or half-step.

As an added benefit, the same technique can be applied to the keyboard's brightness settings, with the Option-Shift modifier once more dividing the adjustment into quarter increments.

AUDIO INPUT SELECTION

If you have several sound-producing devices and accessories connected to the Mac, selecting the volume icon in the menu bar could also display a list of audio outputs. While this does enable users to rapidly establish an alternative audio output—for example, utilizing speakers from a connected display instead of those on the Mac or MacBook—it does not apply to audio inputs.

The volume control slider will disappear when you click the volume icon while holding down Option, and the audio output choices will jump to the top. Instead of showing outputs, the menu will show all of the Mac's audio inputs that are currently in use while also highlighting the selected input.

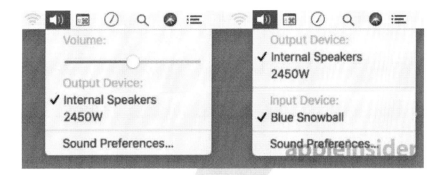

Just as for changing the outputs, clicking a different input in this menu will switch over to that specific device.

CHAPTER EIGHT
EXPANDING HORIZONS WITH MACBOOK ACCESSORIES

ESSENTIAL ACCESSORIES FOR THE MACBOOK

A strong machine is THE MACBOOK. Apple's laptops can perform a variety of tasks, whether you're using a MacBook Air for online surfing and emailing or a MacBook Pro for graphically demanding tasks like video editing and 3D modeling. But I advise adding certain extras to the mix to improve your experience.

Whatever MacBook you choose or the task you're using it for, a variety of accessories, including laptop stands, keyboards, charging bricks, and external screens, may be paired with your machine. The greatest MacBook accessories for streamlining your workflow and maximizing your computer's capabilities are those listed above. There are countless attachments, so this is by no means a comprehensive list.

CHARGING ADAPTERS

Although MacBooks now have better battery life, you should always have a backup charger with you. The one that comes standard in the package is large and can only recharge one device at once.

LAPTOP CASES AND SLEEVES

It doesn't take much to scratch or ding the aluminum on a MacBook. It's smart to get a laptop case or sleeve to keep it safe.

- Incase Hardshell Case Dots (16-inch MacBook Pro)
- Speck Smartshell Case (14-inch MacBook Pro)

- A Leather Sleeve: Harber London Magnetic Envelope Sleeve for MacBooks

HUBS AND DOCKS

Invest in a USB hub or dock if the few ports on your MacBook Air or older MacBook Pro bother you. The inexpensive dongles known as hubs come with additional USB ports, SD card readers, and a headphone jack. Because they are bigger, include more ports in more varieties (such Ethernet), and sometimes have their own power source, docks are designed to be utilized at a desk.

- Twelve South StayGo Mini
- Plugable USB-C Triple Display Docking Station

IF YOU HAVE AN IPHONE

Anker 637 Magnetic Charging Station

Trying to get rid of the desk power strip? Look no farther than the MagGo 637 from Anker. The front MagSafe wireless charger may be used to power your iPhone, while the back of the device has three AC outlets, two USB-C connectors, and two USB-A ports. You can charge a MacBook with one of those USB-C connections since it has a 65 watt output, making it an all-in-one charging station in a little sphere.

KEYBOARDS

It's great, but not required, to spend more money on a nicer keyboard if you spend a lot of time at a desk. especially if you want a mechanical keyboard for a more tactile experience.

- Apple Magic Keyboard with Touch ID and Numeric Keypad
- Logitech MX Mechanical Mini for Mac

MOUSE

For the most comfortable experience, a decent mouse is essential. If you really appreciate the trackpad on your MacBook, I've got you covered with an external trackpad as well as an ergonomic choice (to prevent wrist discomfort).

- Logitech Lift for Mac
- Apple Magic Trackpad 2

LAPTOP STANDS

You may avoid craning your neck to look at the screen by resting your MacBook on a laptop stand.

- ObVus Solutions Laptop Tower Stand
- Nnewvante Laptop Stand

DESK MATS

Your office doesn't really need a desk mat, but it looks great. It may also make things appear a little more tidy and attractive. For anyone utilizing an external mouse, they can also serve as a mousepad.

- Grovemade Wool Felt Desk Pad
- Satechi Dual-Sided Eco-Leather Deskmate

EXTERNAL STORAGE SOLUTIONS AND BACKUPS

Buying an external drive to add more capacity for all of your business data, personal files, films, and games is always a smart option because upgrading the storage in Macs has never been simple. Furthermore, you should always keep an external disk handy so that you can create Time Machine backups in case something goes wrong.

The best alternative is modern solid-state disks (SSD), which are incredibly quick, dependable, and small. In contrast, the same amount of money may be used to purchase a 4TB basic desktop hard drive with a USB interface. SSDs are still rather costly, with 1TB drives costing roughly $100/£150 (drives with high-speed Thunderbolt connections tend to be more expensive). Although hard drives are slower than SSDs, they are still the most cost-effective alternative if you require a lot of storage for your crucial data and backups.

There are also many options, including desktop drives with extremely big capacity if you truly need a lot of storage and small, portable hard drives made for laptop use. Other advantages that some hard drives provide include built-in docks with several Thunderbolt and USB connections and the option to open the disk's shell and replace the drive inside for an immediate upgrade.

SEAGATE ULTRA TOUCH 2023

PROS

- Competitive price
- 2TB, 4TB or 5TB storage
- Password protection and encryption

CONS

- Average performance
- Larger and heavier than original model

LACIE MOBILE DRIVE 2022

PROS

- Competitive price
- LaCie's ToolKit app

CONS

- Not the fastest hard drive available

CHAPTER NINE

TIPS AND TRICK IN MAC OS VENTURA

On your Mac, did you recently install macOS Ventura? Or perhaps you're considering installing the most recent MacOS version and downloading Ventura, and you just want to check what the more interesting features and tricks for MacOS 13 are. Then have a look at some of these fantastic new features that the Mac now has access to thanks to the Ventura release..

MERGE CALENDARS IN MACOS VENTURA

People begin restructuring their life, including calendars, around this time of year. You might need to integrate a number of iCloud calendars as part of that endeavor. This is the procedure.

When you set up email accounts on your device, several calendars are created. After logging in, iOS will provide you with a checkbox asking if you wish to import calendars.

Adding calendars you believe could be beneficial might potentially result in you having many calendars. You're looking at five or six pointless calendars before the end of the year.

There are a few ways to combine calendars, but Mac is the only platform that supports it. Now that you have your PC, let's combine several calendars.

CALENDAR MERGING

To merge calendars as quickly and effectively as you can, follow these steps.

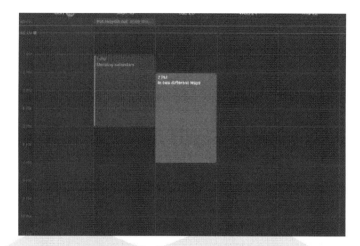

- Launch the Mac's Calendar application. The left side of the screen should display all of your calendars. If not, select Show Calendar List from the View menu.

- Use the right click button to integrate one calendar with another. Choose which calendar you want to integrate with by selecting integrate.

- The previous calendar will be deleted by the app, and a notice will inform you that the events will merge with the new one. Tap Merge.

This technique of combining calendars transfers all events to the new calendar; however, the prior calendar cannot be restored. The following steps will help you build an export file that serves as a backup in case you need to save that data for any reason.

USE 'NEW FOLDER WITH SELECTION' FEATURE IN MACOS VENTURA

Apple enhanced the Finder's New Folder With Selection function in macOS Big Sur. Here are its functions and how to utilize it.

Contextual popup menus have been a feature of the macOS Finder for years. Anywhere on the Desktop, by using the control or right mouse button, you may get a menu with various helpful options, including New Folder, Get Info, Move to Trash, and others.

However, as with macOS Big Sur, Apple introduced a nice new option to the popup menu that appears when Control-clicking on objects that are selected in the Finder: New Folder With Selection.

The New Folder menu option in the Finder changes to New Folder With Selection if you Control-click or right-click on two or more objects to choose them. When you choose that menu option, a new folder is instantly created in your current location, complete with a cute little hop animation, and the objects you've chosen are moved into it all at once.

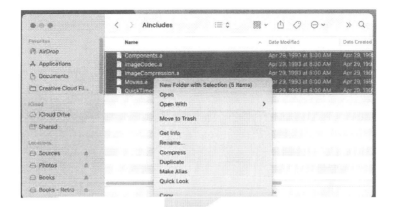

"NEW FOLDER WITH SELECTION" IN MACOS VENTURA

- Choose two or more items from the Desktop or any Finder window.

- Click or right-click on them while depressing the Control key.

- From the pop-up menu, select "New Folder with Selection".

All of your chosen objects are visible when you open that folder and are prepared for opening, sorting, or renaming:

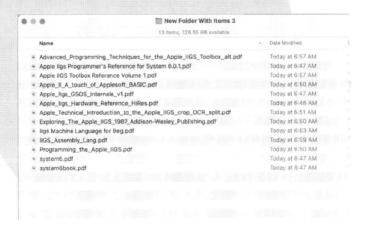

This small new feature saves a ton of time since it eliminates the need to press Command-Shift-N twice to create a folder and then a second and third time to pick and drag objects into it.

The Finder even chooses the folder's name for you once it has been created, ready for you to type a new name for it.

When used in the same situation, the new menu item may likewise be found on the Finder's "File" menu. However, the fact that you can utilize it with just one click on the Desktop without having to go the "File" menu is great.

You'll wonder how you ever managed without the new Finder contextual menu command after using it for the first time. The new command really becomes strangely addictive after a few uses; there is power in being able to quickly move a sizable number of files into a new folder.

Hopefully, Apple will understand in the future that the contextual menu for the Finder might benefit from having a lot more things. The menu hasn't changed much since the Finder of the 1990s, but there is a ton more functionality that might be included to speed up processes.

USE BACKGROUND SOUNDS IN MACOS VENTURA

You may unwind and focus with the aid of this less well-known background noises option in macOS Ventura, which can boost your workstation productivity. Here's how to configure it.

Long hours of studying or working from home might be stressful. You might find that this function helps you relax so you can concentrate on your current activity.

This could be helpful if you want to unwind and relax after a stressful day. You could at least mentally go to the beach with the aid of your Mac.

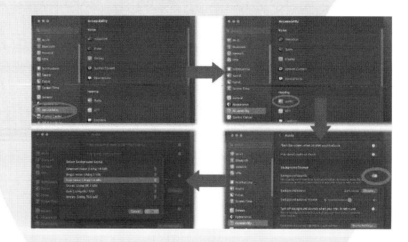

- Select Accessibility from the System Settings menu.
- Select Audio by clicking on Hearing.
- Select "Background Sounds" under the heading "Background Sounds."
- To download a high-quality version of a sound to your Mac, select Choose, then click the Download button next to its name. Additionally, you can check how much room each sound would use on your Mac.

QUIT ALL MAC APPS AT ONCE

It might be annoying to close each program separately when you've been working on your Mac for a while and have several open. Here's how to quickly dismiss every open app.

Even while you can shut down your Mac and stop all of your open programs, you won't want to keep restarting it as you go from one important activity to another.

A shortcut is the most convenient way to dismiss all of your apps at once if you frequently wish to do this. Here's how to use macOS Ventura to quickly dismiss every open program on your computer.

It is simple and only requires one step to create the shortcut. Here's how to make a shortcut to simultaneously dismiss all of your Mac's applications.

- On your Mac, launch Shortcuts.
- To create a new Shortcut, click the Plus button in the application's top right corner.
- Enter "Quit" in the search box on the right side of the screen.
- From the search results, choose "Quit App" under the Scripting section.
- After adding the action, choose "App" from the action prompt.
- Click "All Apps" in the drop-down menu.
- Select the applications you wish to keep running when other apps are closed by clicking on the "Except" wording of the Shortcut.
- Give your shortcut a name and a symbol to help others remember it.
- Click the red traffic icon to close the shortcut.

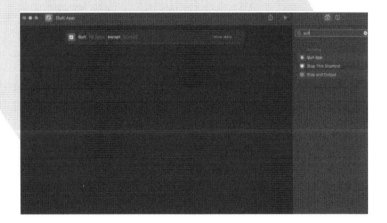

If you have any unsaved documents, the app's icon will bounce in the Dock and the Shortcut will continue to run even when all programs terminate instantaneously while it is active. Until you manually close the unsaved documents, the Shortcuts Stop icon remains Play.

Once the Shortcut is activated, you cannot change your mind. All applications will terminate, with the exception of those that contain unfinished documents. This includes background programs like TextExpander and Keyboard Maestro.

However, the Shortcut may be modified to include a prompt that asks you if you're sure you want to launch it. While creating the shortcut, look for "Ask for Input" under "Scripting" to discover that option.

Using the Shortcuts app, two-finger-click on this shortcut and choose "Add to Dock" to add it to your dock. Running the functionality will become simpler and more available as a result.

CUSTOMIZE THE DOCK

You may alter a variety of settings to modify the macOS Dock's appearance and functionality, which can improve how you use the macOS UI component. Here is how you can get to them.

Go to System Settings->Desktop & Dock from the Apple menu in the macOS menubar to adjust the Dock in macOS. At the top of this settings window are the majority of the Dock-related items:

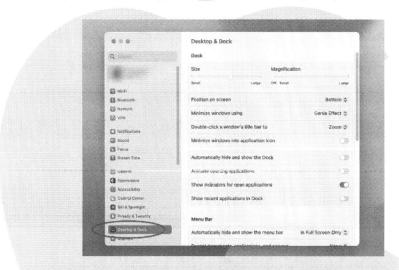

Two sliders are located at the top of the Desktop & Dock window. When you mouse over the Dock, one determines its size and the other determines how magnified it will be.

The Finder will shrink the size of the icons to their lowest size to fit everything in if you jam a lot of programs into the Dock.

You may also completely disable magnification to prevent the icons from shifting as you mouse over them.

A popup menu that moves the Dock's location onscreen follows. You have three options: Left, Bottom, or Right; Bottom is macOS's out-of-the-box default.

When you click the yellow minimize buttons in windows, the animation that is used to shrink Finder windows into the Dock is controlled by the following item, Minimize windows utilizing. The options are Genie or Scale.

When you double-click a window's title bar, you may choose what happens to the window as a result. You can disable this option, enlarge the window, or reduce it.

If the following option, Minimize window into application icon, is enabled, Finder will minimize windows into their parent applications and add them to popup menus when you click the yellow minimize button on a window. By Control-clicking or right-clicking the app's icon in the Dock, you may open the smaller window.

Automatically conceal and reveal By default, the Dock is hidden; however, if you move your cursor over the screen's edge where you want the Dock to appear, it will become visible. This feature allows users to hide and expose the Dock at will with a simple mouse-over for those who believe it to be an obstruction and a screen-blocker.

When animated launching apps is enabled, when an app is started its icon will move up and down in the Dock. Turning off the startup animation will improve responsiveness.

When an application is running, the Dock will show a little dot beneath it when the option to show indications for open programs is selected. It can be useful to be able to quickly determine which programs are open by looking at the Dock.

When you select Show Recent Applications in the Dock menu, the Trash and the right side of the Dock are filled with recently used but closed programs.

We won't discuss the other options because they mostly only affect the Desktop and not the Dock.

SNAP BACK TO YOUR SAFARI SEARCH RESULTS

Let's say you want to research a subject online, so you enter a search term or phrase in Safari's URL bar. You click the first link that appears in the list of results because it seems intriguing. You click another link regarding a comparable subject on the website you were sent to. Then you decide to click on another site when it catches your eye. Before you know it, you've gone down a rabbit hole of clicks and links without learning anything about what you were originally looking for. This happens when you are sidetracked by another unrelated topic.

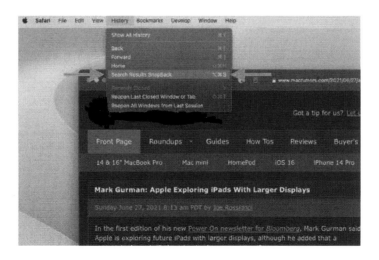

The solution is Safari SnapBack if it sounds similar. It saves you from having to laboriously click the previous page button several times to get back to your first search results or from having to dig through your web history to find the beginning of your most recent online ramble. Under History -> Search Results in Safari's menu bar, you may access it. SnapBack is an option, however using the Command-Option-S keyboard shortcut is preferable.

The SnapBack menu option will be grayed out if you clicked a link that launched a new tab and then continued browsing in that tab since SnapBack only functions if your errant surfing took place in the same tab that you used to start the search. Additionally, you must do the search using Safari's address bar or the webpage for the search engine that Safari is configured to use.

CHAPTER TEN
EXPLORING MACOS VENTURA'S ADVANCED FEATURES

L ike with any other system software update, loads of stuff fly under the radar.

COPY TEXT FROM PAUSED VIDEOS

Copying text from photos was made possible with the release of macOS Monterey. Ventura goes a step farther by enabling text copying from stopped movies. All native software, including QuickTime Player, Apple TV, and Quick Look, are compatible with the feature. Even while playing videos in Safari, it functions.

So, the next time you want to copy text from a video, merely stop it, pick the word or phrase with your cursor, and then choose Copy from the Control-click menu.

GENERATE REAL-TIME AUDIO CAPTIONS

On your Mac, you may create real-time subtitles for system or microphone noises if you're deaf, hard of hearing, or just wish to watch a movie with the level turned down.

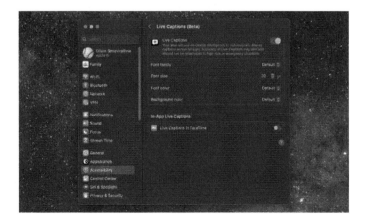

Open the Apple menu and go to System Settings > Accessibility > Live Captions (Beta) to activate Live Captions to start using this accessibility feature.

INSTALL SECURITY UPDATES WITHOUT A RESTART

Updates are crucial, particularly when defending your Mac against security threats. However, they take a long time to install and cause frequent restarts, which might impede your work.

Because of this, Apple deploys security updates separately from normal updates in macOS Ventura. There are no reboots involved and everything takes place in the background.

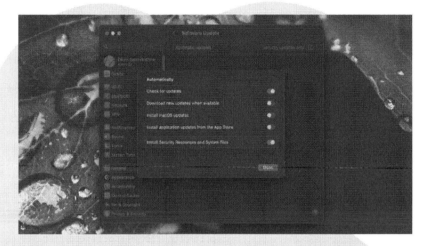

Although the option is turned on by default, to be sure, navigate to System Settings > General > Software Update > Automatic updates, and make sure the switch next to Install Security Responses and System Files is turned on.

SET ALARMS WITH THE NEW CLOCK APP

Do you want to set an alarm? You're not required to pull out your iPhone. Use macOS Ventura's new Clock app in its instead. You may set up one or more alarms from the Alarm tab by going to Launchpad > Clock.

The World Clock, Stopwatch, and Timer are among the features present in Clock for macOS that are comparable to those found in its iOS and iPadOS counterparts.

PLAY RELAXING BACKGROUND SOUNDS

Forget searching YouTube for music to play if you want to cover up grating outside noises or have tinnitus. Instead, you may activate serene background sounds straight from the Accessibility settings in macOS Ventura.

To choose a sound, go to System Settings > Accessibility > Audio and click the Choose option. Then start playing it by turning on the option next to Background noises. To change the audio level without changing the system volume, use the slider next to Background noises volume.

UNDO SEND EMAILS AND MESSAGES

The next email you send that you later discover needs an addition or modification can be revoked. Within 15 seconds, tap the Undo Send button in the lower left corner of the Mail app's display to reopen the message in draft mode.

The Messages app is the same, except you have 15 minutes to cancel a text. To cancel sending a message, just Control-click the message bubble. You may now modify messages in Messages in addition to using Undo Send.

LOCK THE HIDDEN PHOTOS FOLDER

Anyone who is familiar with the Mac's Photos software may browse through the Hidden photo album in a snap. That was the situation previously, at least.

The Hidden folder in macOS Ventura is protected by Touch ID or your user account password. You don't have to permanently delete private photographs after deleting them because even the Recently Deleted folder is secured.

If Hidden and Recently Deleted don't have a lock icon next to them in the Photos app's sidebar, go to Photos > Settings > General and turn on the Use Touch ID or password setting.

USE QUICK LOOK IN SPOTLIGHT SEARCH

Being integrated directly into Spotlight Search in macOS Ventura makes Quick Look an even more useful tool. Simply choose the item you wish to see in the search results using the arrow keys, then hit Space.

ADD FILTERS TO YOUR FOCUS PROFILES

With the release of macOS Monterey, Do Not Disturb changed into Focus. Focus is now much better since Focus Filters allow you to establish limitations within individual programs.

To create a unique filter for any Focus profile, navigate to System Settings >Focus and click the Focus Filter option. For instance, while the Work Focus is active, you may select the Mail mailbox from which you wish to receive notifications.

REMOVE BACKGROUNDS FROM IMAGES

Machine learning algorithms included into macOS Ventura are capable of identifying and duplicating topics inside photographs. It functions in Quick Look, Photos, and Safari and is always active.

Simply control-click a photo, choose Copy Subject, and then paste the result wherever you want the subject to appear. The image topic can alternatively be saved as a PNG file.

RECEIVE SEVERE WEATHER ALERTS

The weather application on macOS Ventura is superb. It's entertaining to use and provides a ton of information without being overpowering. It can also give you notifications when danger is nearby if you live in a region that is prone to extreme weather.

Check the option next to Severe Weather Alerts after opening the Weather app and choosing Weather > Settings from the navigation bar.

BETTER PASSWORD SUGGESTIONS IN SAFARI

You don't have to use the impossible-to-type string of nonsense that the browser generates by default when establishing passwords in Safari.

Instead, use the Other Options drop-down to access a number of other settings. The default password can be changed, a simpler version chosen, or a password devoid of special characters chosen.

MERGE DUPLICATE IMAGES IN PHOTOS

Duplicating photos and movies is possible with the Photos app on macOS Ventura. On the sidebar of the program, pick Duplicates. Next, choose Merge "X" items over collections of items with a similar appearance. Long-term, expect to save a significant amount of local and iCloud storage.

CONCLUSION

Although expensive, MacBooks now rank among the most feature-rich computers available. Despite their high price. It might be really intimidating attempting to get a hold of your new machine if you're new to the macOS ecosystem. With the release of macOS, 13 Ventura, which has so many innovative and interesting features, the MacBook Air has risen to the top of our list of the finest laptops available right now.

This book is the ideal option if you want to get the most out of your new MacBook, whether you bought it for yourself as a treat for business, school, or a passion project or received it as a present.

This Mac user's handbook only scratches the surface of the topics available. You'll learn more about what your Mac is capable of as you use it more frequently. There are countless alternatives, therefore the greatest advise I can give you is to just take pleasure in using your Mac.

DO NOT GO YET; ONE LAST THING TO DO

If you enjoyed this book or found it useful, I'd be very grateful if you'd post a short review on Amazon. Your support does make a difference, and I read all the reviews personally so I can get your feedback and make this book even better.

Thanks again for your support!

INDEX

Made in the USA
Las Vegas, NV
27 August 2023

76702346R00061